3·20·79

inside
powerlifting

terry todd

cbi Contemporary Books, Inc.
Chicago

To Jan, who brought me back.

Copyright © 1978 by Terry Todd
All rights reserved
Published by Contemporary Books, Inc.
180 North Michigan Avenue, Chicago, Illinois 60601
Manufactured in the United States of America
Library of Congress Catalog Card Number: 77-23710
International Standard Book Number: 0-8092-7858-8 (cloth)
0-8092-7854-5 (paper)

Published simultaneously in Canada by
Beaverbooks
953 Dillingham Road
Pickering, Ontario L1W 1Z7
Canada

contents

acknowledgments

I wish to thank Peary and Mabel Rader of *Iron Man* magazine and Bob Hoffman, John Terpak, and John Grimek of *Muscular Development* and *Strength and Health* magazines for allowing me permission to use certain of their photographs.

In addition, I'd like to thank my nine subjects for being so generous with their time, information, and even their private collections of photographs. Without their help, there would have been no book.

introduction

To qualify is to make the grade. You have to qualify for everything today. In the next few pages I'd like to explain why Terry Todd qualifies to write in the way only he can about champions of powerlifting.

THEIR DAY'S WORK done in the gym and their minds on barbequed ribs and beer, four big Texans pose for photographer Mike Graham at the Texas Athletic Club. From left to right: Terry Todd, former Superheavyweight Powerlifting Champion and world record holder; Jan Todd, first woman to exceed 1,000 pounds in the powerlifts; Doug Young, two-time World Champion in the 242-pound class; and Robert Young, starting offensive guard for the St. Louis Cardinals and the strongest man in pro football.

I truly feel that one of the main reasons our sport has grown so rapidly in the decade and a half since it began is because of Terry Todd. In the early 1960s, when the sport was born, Todd was there. In 1964, when the first national championships were held, Todd was there, winning the superheavies and outdistancing the winner in the bodyweight class below by 375 pounds. In 1965, when the time finally came for someone to break the deadlift record of the legendary Bob Peoples which had stood for almost 20 years, Todd was there, doing the breaking.

Todd started as an Olympic lifter back in the days before there *were* any powerlift meets and he was a good one. He entered his first Olympic contest when he was an undergraduate at the University of Texas. At U. T. he had a full scholarship in tennis, even though he weighed 240 pounds by the time he was a sophomore, and represented his school in the National Intercollegiate Championships.

TODD STARTS TO smile as he pulls up 730 pounds to exceed Bob Peoples' world record which had stood for 15 years.

His tennis coach noticed his growing size and said no way to the weights, but Todd kept on lifting anyway, often entering contests under aliases such as Andy Hepburn or Doug Anderson. Finally, he gave up his athletic scholarship in his junior year because his coach pestered him so much about losing weight. After leaving tennis, he was approached by some U. T. football coaches who knew of his great strength and speed and who wanted him to try out for the team, but by then he was hooked on the iron and he turned them down.

He kept getting bigger and pushing hard with the weights, doing all kinds of exercises, and lifting in a few Olympic-type contests as he got heavier and stronger. He was National Intercollegiate Champion and Junior National Champion in 1963, and by then he was probably the strongest man in the world, overall. Of course there were a few lifters in Europe and a couple in the U. S. who could snatch and clean and jerk more than Todd but none of them could pull as much weight as high as he could or press as much as strictly.

BENT FORWARD ROWING always played a big role in Todd's exercise programs. Although he used as much as 500 pounds for five repetitions, he is shown here with "only" 455. *(Lower right)* Todd's shoulders, chest, and arms were among the largest in the history of the iron game. Although he used straps to assist his grip when he did more than one repetition, he once pulled 1,025 pounds from this position with his hands alone. *(Left)* His face showing the strain of the awesome weight, Todd pulls up 785 pounds, 40 pounds over his own world record.

I've talked to people who were around in those days and who saw him train, and these people say that when you watched him lift alongside such heavyweights as Norbert Schemansky, Gary Gubner, and Bob Bednarski, there was no question that the big man from Texas was stronger. Even the almost mythical Paul Anderson never bench pressed or power cleaned or deadlifted as much as Todd, and he couldn't close the handles on a heavy-duty gripper that Todd could shut eight times with either hand.

In short, Todd was a terrifically powerful athlete who was probably kept from winning an Olympic gold medal by the enormous size of his upper arms and forearms. They were so big that they kept him from being able to double his arms up enough so that he could hold the bar comfortably across his shoulders. And the bigger and stronger he got the more trouble he had "racking" the bar on his shoulders; so he finally gave up on Olympic lifting and concentrated on the sport which is the subject of this book. (In Olympic lifting, the lifts are the snatch and the clean and jerk. In powerlifting, the lifts are the squat, the bench press, and the deadlift.)

To give you an idea of just how big and strong Todd was, take a look at the following list of measurements and strength feats I got from old magazines and from people who trained with Todd when he was competing.

Height: 6 feet, 2½ inches
Weight: 340 pounds
Chest: 61 inches normal
Thighs: 36½ inches
Biceps: 22¾ inches cold
Waist: 46 inches
Forearm: 17 inches straight

Seated Press (no support for back): 385 pounds
Strict Press off the rack: 400 pounds
Push Press: 475 pounds
Power Clean: 405 × 3 (no straps), 450 × 1
Power Snatch: 300 × 3 (no straps)
Front Squat: 600 × 3
Back Squat: 625 × 10 for 3 sets and 700 × 5
Deadlift: 750 × 3 (no straps), 800 × 1
Incline Bench Press: 500 pounds
Partial Front Squat: 1,200 pounds
Partial Deadlift (from just above knees): 1,025 pounds (no straps)
High Pull onto belt: 550 pounds
Bent Forward Rowing: 500 pounds × 5

Most of the above were no doubt world records when they were made—some probably *still* are—but they were made in practice, in the gym, just for the pleasure of handling big weights. To me, his greatest strength was in his hands and arms. How about a strict reverse curl with 175? Or pinch gripping two 35-pound plates smooth side out and then *cleaning* them? Or maybe 20 reps with 250 pounds in the wrist curl? I'd bet my bottom dollar that back then no one alive could have beaten him at arm wrestling. Actually, as far as I'm concerned no one could beat him *now*. People told me that they saw him do various leverage stunts with big sledge hammers that they simply couldn't believe.

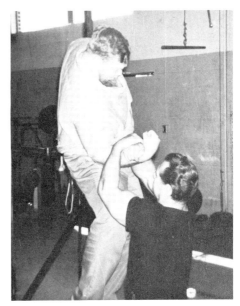

WELL BELOW PARALLEL with the world's first official 700-pound squat (actual weight 710) at the first Junior National Powerlifting Championships in 1965. *(Below)* Although this snapshot leaves a lot to be desired, it shows Todd's amazing arm strength. He is standing on a leg extension machine and 210-pound John Grimek is being "curled" by Todd's 23-inch right arm.

Olympic lifting's loss was powerlifting's gain, and by the time he finished his course work for his Doctor of Philosophy degree at U.T., he was ready to go to York, Pennsylvania, to take over the managing editorship of *Strength and Health* magazine and to usher in the first legitimately national meet. By 1964 he had already been the first man to officially total 1,600 pounds in the three powerlifts, the first to total 1,700 pounds, and the first to total 1,800 pounds,

TODD IS MUCH taller and broader than the rotund Paul Anderson. Between them they were stronger in just about every way in the mid-1960's than anyone else in the world.(Right) The big Doc had to hump it a bit to pull an 800 he once took during an exhibition in California.

and he went on to become the first to officially reach 1,900, and the first to unofficially reach 2,000 and 2,100. His best official lifts were 720 in the squat, 515 in the bench press, and 742 in the deadlift, but in the gym he was good for 775, 535, and 800.

It was a lucky thing for powerlifting that a man like Todd was there to get the sport started right. It wasn't only his strength and physical size that helped make the sport legitimate; it was his personality, intelligence, and charisma. With Todd in the sport, no one could say that powerlifters were a bunch of dumb, clumsy misfits who couldn't make it anywhere else. Having him around and hearing him talk made you proud to be a powerlifter.

In 1967, after dominating the sport for four years and setting 15 world records, Todd retired to concentrate on his university teaching, but he returned to the sport in 1971 through his writing of instructional articles in *Muscular Development* and his reporting for *M. D.* and *Iron Man* of the results of the major powerlifting meets around the world. His unique description of powerlifting and powerlifters have literally changed the sport. Rarely, if ever, has a sports journalist been able to influence in a major way the sport he writes about, but that's exactly what Todd has done. I can say flatly that I would have retired in 1974 had it not been for his coverage of a couple of key meets. He put things in a new perspective for me and changed my attitude 100 percent. His words made me realize how much the game really meant to me.

During the years Todd was establishing himself as a university professor, the game seemed to dwindle a bit in terms of class and respect—he was missed by all of us. But thank God he's back. Later in the book he writes that I have class, but trust me when I say that what class I do have rubbed off from the big Doc.

IN 1965, AT the first truly official National Powerlifting Championships, the winners were Wilbur Miller, third; Terry Todd, first; and Gene Roberson, second. *(Right)* Back in the mid-1960's, just before Robert "Bubba" Young was going up to play his first year of pro football, he trained with Todd, who scuffles with him here outside the Texas Athletic Club. Todd, on the left, weighed 325 and Young weighed 285.

When he shows up at a lifting event, that event becomes more important, because lifters know that what they do with him watching will live on through his accurate, honest words. His presence helps lifters extend themselves—they make lifts they wouldn't otherwise be capable of just to see how Todd will write about it. He writes with drama, with an understanding of the *adventure* of big-time lifting, and with a perfect feel for down-home humor.

I told Bob Hoffman, sponsor of most of the big powerlift meets for the last dozen years, about this introduction and he had this to say about Todd's contributions to the sport.

> Terry Todd is a fine young man whom I've known for many years. His efforts both on and off weightlifting platforms have helped to build the sport tremendously. He was our first national champion in powerlifting, and he was one of the strongest men I've ever seen. Also, his writings on the sport are the best anyone has ever done. He has an amazing memory about all the oldtimers and this gives him a good perspective on the game.

Another man who has made use of Todd's talents through the years is Peary Rader, who published the first of Todd's 100-plus articles in *Iron Man* way back in 1961, and who saw him lift many times. Peary said,

> I have known Terry Todd for many years and consider him one of the leading authors and teachers of weightlifting in the country with an interesting style of writing and a knowledge of weightlifting unexcelled by anyone else. Having been a world champion himself, he has an awareness of the whole field, not

just from the viewpoint of an author and teacher but also from the competitor's viewpoint. In addition to his great knowledge in the field which gives him great accuracy in reporting events, he also has a contagious enthusiasm that makes his work interesting to everyone whether they be the general public or the dedicated lifting participant.

Believe me when I say that powerlifters all over the world share the opinion of Todd held by Hoffman and Rader. Most people in the game feel that Todd knows as much about powerlifting as anyone does and agree that he writes about it much better than anyone else ever has. So, it seems only right that he should be the man to write the first book about powerlifting.

I'm a personal friend of every one of the people Todd has chosen to include in the following pages, and I think that if I'd been the one doing the choosing I'd have picked the same athletes he did. All the people he picked are known to be thoughtful, hardworking trainers as well as tough, successful competitors. All of them are world champions, world-record holders, or both. I'm proud to be among them.

I almost feel that Todd made a mistake by not including a chapter on himself, because I feel that he could be one of the top few supers in the world even today if he wanted to train hard for six months or so. But his time is precious, I know. He and his amazing wife, Jan, live on a small working farm in Nova Scotia, where they grow almost all of their food with their team of draft horses, and raise mastiff and bull-mastiff dogs.

Lately, he's been working with Jan as she trained to become the first woman to total over 1,000 pounds in the three powerlifts. She made it last week with an official 1,042, and he recorded the details of her decision to train for strength and the methods she used to become the strongest woman in the world in one of the last chapters. To me, that chapter alone is worth the price of the book.

With his writing on lifting and other fields, his farmwork, his coaching of Jan and other lifters, and his professorship at Dalhousie University, he's not left with the time to train as a world-class powerman, but what a treat it would be to see him step out to the chalkbox one more time. To be honest, it wouldn't surprise me, but even if he never touches another weight, coaches another lifter, or writes another word about our sport, he's already qualified as an immortal in powerlifting. Last year, he was the first retired lifter chosen for induction into the Powerlifting Hall of Fame. Not only has he *qualified*, he's gone a few steps beyond onto the elite plateau reserved for legends. He has been our guiding light and inspiration since powerlifting began, and I know I speak for powerlifters everywhere in hoping that we continue to benefit from his remarkable presence for years to come.

Larry Pacifico
June 1977

STUFFED AND HAPPY after tackling the Yorktowne Hotel Seafood Buffet are Doug and Judy Young, Terry and Jan Todd, and Don and Cindy Reinhoudt.

chapter 1

POWERLIFTS AND POWERLIFTERS

I am convinced that the only people worthy of consideration in this world are the truly unusual ones. For the common folk are like leaves on a tree, and live and die unnoticed.

—The Scarecrow from
The Marvelous Land of Oz
by L. Frank Baum

POWERLIFTING PAST AND PRESENT

As I sit here by my garden, watching my heavy horses graze the green grass, I feel a sense of real reluctance and sadness as I begin the end of this book on the sport of strength. This is so because I realize that when I am done my interests and commitments will lead me to other things and the concentration I have focused on powerlifting for the past few months will be diffused. I will not, of course, *leave* powerlifting or *forget* it, even if I wanted to or could, but I doubt that I will ever again return to it so completely. Never again will it possess me as it has lately and as it did even more so during my years of competition.

I imagine that the wellspring of my reluctance and sadness is the fact that the unsparing passion which I brought to the sport when I first began it provided me with what I now can see were the happiest times of my life. From what I've seen through the years, this is true of many serious athletes. I remember Ronnie Ray, one of the founders of powerlifting in the 1960s and now a millionaire gym owner, turning to me last year at the Nationals and saying, "You know, I've made a lot of money, but in all my life my happiest

MARVIN PHILLIPS AND Doug Young realized how hard Don Reinhoudt had tried to deadlift 900 pounds and how much he wanted to make it. So when he failed, they were right there consoling him and sharing in his sadness. Only those who have trained as hard as these men train can understand what the big lifts mean.

times by far were those when I was in top shape, humping that iron."

People have often asked me how I was able to push myself with such relentlessness in a sport in which there was no monetary reward and very little publicity outside the lifting magazines, and the question always brings to mind the remark a track coach once made about long-distance running. "When you see them late in the evening, often in the rain," he said, "driving themselves to run just one more mile, you should never, never pity them, for they are the happiest of men." There is a sense in which this total dedication to a sport—the sort of total dedication manifested in the lives of the nine athletes in this book—tends to blur the clarity and diminish the importance of everything else in a person's life.

Whether this is ultimately good or bad for the individual involved or for the society in which he or she lives is a fascinating question, but it is not the subject of this book. Instead, the true subject of this book is the lives of the nine people who have been good enough to share their knowledge and insight and background with me. Through their lives run the common threads of sacrifice and singlemindedness—the two universal traits of world-class athletes—binding them together in their dedication to what can only be called excellence.

During the months that I've talked to these people, corresponded with them, and gone over the details of their lives, I've felt myself being drawn again into that intense cocoon of absorbed commitment that I thought I'd left behind forever when I retired in 1967. For me, doing this book has been like a homecoming, a going back to simpler, less troubled times. And although my life is now lived so that I can afford no more than a visit, it was enough to have gone back this once, especially in such damn fine company.

From the outset, I decided not to write powerlifting's first book completely out of my own experiences because I wanted to provide not simply information which was *adequate;* I wanted to provide a breadth of material which would come as close as possible to defining what the sport offered and what it demanded. My aim was not necessarily to write an instructional book, though this certainly is one, but to use the lives of the athletes themselves and the sport of powerlifting to distill the essence of all sport.

In order to do this I asked nine people I had come to know well through the years—nine people who are the aristocracy of powerlifting—to work with me to make this book something of which all powerlifters could be proud. To the degree that the book succeeds, most of the credit should go to these nine extraordinary people because they held nothing back. "Secret" routines, one-of-a-kind family album photographs, psychological tactics, personal dietary habits, contest strategy—everything is here. And to the degree that the book fails, lay the blame on me for not being skillful enough to weave the wonderful material I was given into a pattern which would meet the needs of powerlifters everywhere, be they old or young, male or female, novice or veteran.

THE INCOMPARABLE RUSSIAN, Vasily Alexeev, is an Olympic lifter, not a powerlifter. The lift being shown is the clean and jerk, in which he holds the record: 562 pounds. Photo by Klemens.

The fact that "officially" powerlifting is a relatively new sport and has no books of its own increased the pressure I felt to see that nothing was held back. Olympic lifting and bodybuilding, the two other primary sports involving progressive resistance, both have had dozens of books devoted to their various aspects, but, as of mid-1977, powerlifting has had none. In a way this is strange, as powerlifting has already moved well beyond Olympic lifting in popularity throughout the English-speaking world during the past 15 years.

Perhaps one of the chief reasons for powerlifting's rapid gain in public acceptance is that, relative to Olympic lifting, little time has to be spent on technique, as the powerlifts are comparatively simple to perform, strength being their main requirement. The Olympic lifts, on the other hand, require a high degree of flexibility, balance, and coordination, all of which demand proper training for a beginner as well as constant practice. Another cause of powerlifting's popularity may stem from the complex nature of Olympic lifting, for while the physical intricacies of a record clean and jerk are beautiful to a connoisseur, the average person, unable to follow the action and *relate* to the lift, is often unimpressed. But the same person watching the primeval simplicity of a heavy deadlift is unfailingly captivated by the struggle of the lifter and the bending of the bar under the conflicting forces.

Unfortunately, one of the results of this popularity has been a rift between powerlifters and Olympic lifters, an alienation of one group from the other. It puts me in mind of the squabbles I used to hear years ago in Texas between two groups of Baptists, the Hard-Shells and the Foot-Washers. Back then, it always seemed to me that both groups would have been happier, not to mention a good deal closer to God's word, had they concentrated on their similarities rather than

OTHER PEOPLE WHO use weights to develop their strength and musculature are bodybuilders. Shown here is one of the best of a few years ago, Casey Viator.

their differences. These days, I feel the same way about powerlifters and Olympic lifters.

I competed as an Olympic lifter way back in the days before there *were* any powerlift meets in the U.S. Within the past year I watched the Olympic Champions David Rigert and Vasily Alexeev train and then break world records. I even went out to supper with them one night. As wonderful as they are to watch and as impressive as they are in person, I don't see how anyone can seriously try to make a logical case that Alexeev and Rigert are somehow better men than powerlifting's Don Reinhoudt and Larry Pacifico. All *four* are good men—extraordinary men—and they are each the best in their weight class that their respective sports have ever produced.

The point is that Alexeev, Reinhoudt, Rigert, and Pacifico are all *lifters*—each of them develops and maintains his strength by *lifting*. To argue that one form of lifting is better than another is absurd, and I suggest that both Olympic lifters and powerlifters admit this and stop making fools of themselves. You can, after all, *prefer* something without maintaining that your preference is intrinsically better than the preference of someone else. The French writer Francois de La Rochefoucauld put it this way back in the 17th century: "Happiness lies in our tastes, and not in things themselves; a man is happy in doing what he likes, not what others like."

ONE OF THE real stylists in the deadlift is 132-pound world-record holder Eddie Pengelly, who pulled 578 in the 1977 British Championships.

Those for whom happiness is doing or watching the powerlifts, all I can say is that they—we—have chosen a sport which is as basic and ancient as any in the world. Historians suspect that the earliest forms of competitive sport were footraces and tests of strength involving logs and boulders. Picture an early man bending over to get a good handhold on a big chunk of sandstone while his community stood around and urged him on. The muscles of the hands, forearms, back, hips, and legs that would've been used to haul the boulder free of the ground tens of thousands of years ago are the exact same muscles that Don Reinhoudt or

Vince Anello would use today to pull their world-record deadlifts.

Although the three earliest historical records we have of contests of strength are some drawings done on the wall of a funerary chapel at Beni-Hassan in Egypt some 4,500 years ago, some accounts dating back to 1896 B.C. from what are now known as the British Isles, and a wealth of information about the pre-Christian classical period in Greece and Rome, we can be certain that what we now call the deadlift is far older and has been done competitively in one form or another ever since mankind has been far enough advanced to take a breather from either hunting or being hunted. Quite likely one of the reasons for powerlifting's rapid growth, as I said earlier, is its primitive, artless quality. People love it *because* it is uncomplicated, because it is *pure*.

There is a huge block of volcanic rock in what is now Italy which bears the 6th century B.C. inscription, "Eumastas the son of Critobulus lifted me from the ground." There were no *tricks* involved in what Eumastas did and the pride he felt, which was great enough to cause him to carve that inscription, must have been very like the pride I felt the day I broke Bob Peoples' 25-year-old world deadlift record. Tricks have no more place in stone lifting than they do in deadlifting, and if Eumastas was at all like me—and God knows he must have been—that fact was a large part of his pride.

Of course this is not to say that there are no shortcuts in powerlifting because, as this book makes clear, there are. One of these shortcuts, in fact, goes too far, according to some powerlifters. This too-short shortcut is the use of anabolic steroids to increase strength and muscle mass. I was around when steroids—usually methandrostenalone (Dianabol)—began to be used, and I've watched their growth with real fascination. From a "secret" experiment on several members of the 1960 Olympic weightlifting team, the use of these male hormones has spread throughout the athletic world so fast and far that it was estimated by some observers that as many as 30 percent of the male and 20 percent of the female contestants in the Montreal Olympics had used anabolic steroids as part of their preparation for the Games.

Without getting unnecessarily technical, I should explain that the word anabolic refers simply to the building of body tissues and that the word steroid refers to a fat-soluble organic compound. Several decades ago, researchers began to look for a way to separate the anabolic effects of the male sex hormone, testosterone, from its androgenic (masculine-characteristic producing) ones, such as voice deepening, increased hairiness, a stronger sex drive, etc., so that they could treat various types of physical problems without causing over-masculinization.

Their research led to the creation of anabolic steroids which could be administered either orally or by injection, and soon the big drug firms were producing

IN 1978, THE World Powerlifting Championships will be held in Finland, home of Haanu Saarelainen, silver medalist in 1976 as a 242-pounder. As the scorecard behind him shows, there are powerlifters now from all over the world: Canada, Sweden, Japan, India, Zambia. Even the faraway island of Tonga was represented.

them under such trade names as Dianabol, Winstrol, Durabolin, Deca-Durabolin, Anavar, Nilevar, etc. In the beginning they were used to treat such problems as severe burns (because of the tendency of the hormone to promote nitrogen retention), postoperative muscular atrophy, geriatric (aged) debilitation, and cases involving hormonal imbalance. But before long athletes began to realize that if these steroids could strengthen the weak, they might also strengthen the strong. So they jimmied the lock on Pandora's box, and we entered the era of pharmacology.

I use the word "we" advisedly, for I was among the first to take them. I took them quite simply because I believed that they would help my lifting, and there is no question in my mind that they did. Today, if I were to reenter competition, I would take them again. In all honesty I should add that I took them only after reading everything I could find on the subject at the Texas Medical Association Library, only after undergoing a complete physical examination (liver function test, etc.) by the best internist in town, and only as prescribed by my doctor. I wanted to win all right, and I wanted to win bad, but I wasn't stone crazy.

Beginning in the late 1960s and continuing through the 1970s, many articles have been written on the subject in scientific journals. Some of the articles report research which claims that steroids do *not* produce gains in size and/or strength; some of them report research that says they *do* produce such gains; and some of them report research which says they do *only* in the presence of other factors, such as rigorous exercise and a diet rich in protein. One conclusion which *can* be drawn from this conflicting research is

that while steroids may or may not enhance muscular development and strength, they are definitely not a sort of surefire magic potion *guaranteed* to make you strong. If they do help, the help they give is percentagewise quite small. *However*, if we supposed for argument's sake that they produced a gain of only 5 percent in strength, this seemingly small 5 percent translates to 25 pounds when you're in the 500 pound range. In other words, if you were able to deadlift 500, a 5 percent increase in your strength would allow you to deadlift 525. And as contests are often won or lost by only five pounds on the *total* of the three lifts, a 5 percent increase in strength begins to seem monumental. So goes the thinking of those of us who have taken them.

TODD AND HIS team of 2,000-pound draft horses, Don and Cindy (named for the Reinhoudts).

I realize that to have mentioned them at all in this book will cause some people to criticize me, but I felt that it would be dishonest to omit this aspect of powerlifting. I wanted this book to be a truthful one and I have done what I could to make it so, but no one should interpret my remarks about steroids as a recommendation for their use. They are not without their possible dangers, such as cholestatic jaundice, mild hypertension, liver toxicity, suppression of spermatogenesis, and the termination of linear growth as a result of closure of the epiphyses. Anyone contemplating their use should proceed cautiously, *if at all,* under the watchful eye of a physician, preferably a specialist in internal medicine.

As you read through this book, you'll notice that none of the exercise routines and diets of the champions mention any use of steroids. This was done because their use in amateur sport is illegal. I refrained from asking the powerlifters in this book whether or not they took steroids because I didn't want to put them in an awkward or compromised position. Except for Jan, who has never used them, I have no *direct* knowledge that *any* of the men use steroids, but I consider it likely that some of them have done so. However, had steroids never been introduced into heavy athletics, I haven't the slightest doubt that these same lifters would still be the strongest men of their weight in the world. They are, after all, the greatest champions in our sport, and they got where they are through a combination of genetic heritage, will, and good fortune. Pills and injections had very little, *if anything,* to do with it.

As for *other* shortcuts, the pages that follow are full of them. I doubt that ever again will so much personalized material on powerlifting be gathered together in one book. I say this because no longer does the United States dominate the sport as it did in the early days. I can imagine a future in which the world champions in the ten bodyweight classes will come from six or eight different countries. Last year—at the sixth world championships—four of the gold medalists were from the United States, four were from Great Britain, one was from Canada, and one was from Japan. And, for the first time, the United States lost the team championship, bowing to the lifting, coaching, and luck of the wonderful English squad. What this means is that it will be increasingly hard in the future for one person to get to know the best people in the sport as I know the ones whose stories make up this book. Geography, language, and the secretiveness and politics which go hand in hand with the internationalization of any sport will combine to make it almost impossible.

I feel fortunate—undeservedly fortunate—to have been so much a part of the birth and growth of powerlifting and to have been in a position to write the sport's first book. I consider it, as they say, an honor and a privilege and I trust that those of you who read what I have written will feel that I have neither dishonored the sport nor abused the privilege.

I am the teacher of athletes,
He that by me spreads a wider breast than my own proves the width
of my own,
He most honors my style who learns under it to destroy the teacher.
—Walt Whitman, *Leaves of Grass*

ONE OF THE most amazing athletes in the world is Japan's 114-pound world champion, Hideaki Inaba, who can squat over four times his own body weight.

chapter 2
THE SQUAT

The squat, or deep knee bend, is considered by most authorities to be the single greatest exercise in the world for gaining bodyweight. Because of the demands it places on the large muscles of the thighs, hips, and lower back, and because of the deep breathing which occurs when more than three or four repetitions are done, it seems to stimulate muscular growth in a way quite unlike any other movement. Also, it is a cornerstone exercise in any decent program of weight training for athletics because of the power it so quickly builds in the parts of the body which are primarily responsible for running and jumping. It works the hips, thighs, and lower back *as a unit* and, because of this, it is indispensable as a developer of athletic power.

Done no doubt by people all over the world as a daily part of their lives once they began walking upright, the squat in various forms has been done as an exercise at least since the classical period of Greece. Even now, weightless squats in sets of 500 are done by the mudpit wrestlers of India in much the same way they have done them for centuries, and the strength, size, and cardiorespiratory endurance which result have created some of the toughest and most feared grapplers in the history of sport. As a competitive lift, using a barbell for added resistance, full squats are really a product of this century. They began to come to full flower first in Germany, and they were among the contested lifts when Karl Moerke defeated Herman Goerner in

1919 and again in 1920 when Goerner turned the tables on the 5-feet 2-inch Moerke, the man who was probably the first ever to exceed the 600-pound barrier.

Another German, Henry "Milo" Steinborn, brought the lift with him to the U.S. in the 1920s and popularized it here with his remarkable exhibitions of flexibility and strength. From that time until now the lift has continued to prosper as its amazing ability to produce size and strength was ever more clearly recognized. When the squat—usually included as one of the "odd lifts"—began to be contested and the contests turned out to be popular, it was only a matter of time before it would become an official part of the official sport of powerlifting.

Below, through the courtesy of the International Powerlifting Federation, (IPF), I have provided rules governing the performance of the squat. Other aspects of the rules are included in the sections on the bench press and the dead-lift, and in the appendix.

D. Competitive Lifts.
Deep Knee Bend (Squat)

1. The lifter must assume an upright position with the top of the bar not more than one inch below the top of the deltoids, the bar across the shoulders in a horizontal position, hands gripping the bar, feet flat on the platform. Upon removing the bar from the racks, the lifter must move backward to establish his position. He shall wait in this position for the referee's signal, which shall be given as soon as the lifter is motionless and the bar is properly positioned.
2. After the referee's signal, the lifter shall bend the knees and lower the body until the tops of the thighs are below parallel with the platform. The lifter shall recover at will, without double bouncing to an upright position, knees locked, and wait for the referee's signal to replace the bar, which shall be given when the lifter is absolutely motionless. The lifter must make a bona fide attempt to return the bar to the rack.

The tops of the thighs shall be defined as being the point at the hip joint that bends when the body is lowered. This point shall develop a parallel relationship with the top of the knee. This refers to the surface of the leg at the hip joint that bends when the body is lowered.
3. The apparatus used shall be of IPF standards. Padding may be applied to the bar only, but it must not exceed 30 cm. in width and 5 cm. in thickness. The lifter shall remove the bar from the racks preparatory to the lift.
4. The lifter must face the front of the platform.
5. The lifter may not hold the collars, sleeves, or the plates at any time during the performance of the lift. However, the side of the hand may contact the inside of the inner collars.

Causes for Disqualification of the Squat

1. During the lift, failure to wait for the referee's signals.
2. Any change of the position of the hands on the bar.
3. More than one recovery attempt.
4. Failure to assume an upright position at the start and completion of the lift.
5. Failure to lower the body until the tops of the thighs are below parallel.

6. Any shifting of the feet during the performance of the lift.

7. Any shifting of the bar on the body during the performance of the lift.

8. Any touching of the bar by the spotters before the referee's signal.

9. Any raising of the heels or toes.

10. Any touching of the legs with the elbows or upper arms.

MARVIN PHILLIPS

MARV DRIVES UP with his second world record of the night at the 1976 World Championships. This 777.5 was made on his fourth attempt. Note that his thumbs are on top of the bar.

Twenty-five years ago, on a farm in California, a seven-year-old boy was out at the edge of a field with his parents, who were felling some big eucalyptus trees. And as boys will do, he thought he'd see how high he could climb and before anyone knew it he was 60 feet above the ground. And then he fell. Twenty feet before he hit the ground he struck a big limb with the underside of his right arm just below the shoulder and it tore his arm completely off. Today, instead of having been thoroughly blended through the process of dust to dust into the ecosystem of Southern California, that right arm measures 20½ inches around and it's attached to the body of a man who can bench press 500 and who has the best chance of anyone to become the first nonsuperheavyweight to squat with 900 pounds.

The man is Marvin Phillips, 1974 National Champion, policeman, ladies' man, world-record holder in the squat, and ex-one-armed farm boy. Luckily for little Marv, his family lived less than an hour away from one of the most advanced hospitals in the world, and the doctors there were able to take 287 internal stitches and 167 external ones and literally sew his arm back onto his body where it grew and prospered. By the time Marv entered his teens, his right arm was an inch and a half shorter than his left

but it was in good working order; so his dad bought him a 110-pound concrete set of Sears weights and the boy was on his way. He did benches, presses, curls, and squats off and on throughout high school, but it wasn't until he joined the service that he began to train with any seriousness.

Always one for close calls, Marv had two more in the Navy—the first occurred when the destroyer he was on was cut in half one night by an off-course cruiser, with the loss of half the crew. The second happened when he was on *another* destroyer, one which sank 40 miles off the California coast after blowing its experimental boiler. By this time old Marv figured that he and the Navy weren't exactly *suited* for each other; so he shipped out, went back home where he played a little junior college football, and after a couple of years, joined the Pomona police force in 1967.

The funny thing was that although the Pomona P. D. had a powerlifting team, Marv never tried out because he didn't think he had the necessary potential for strength. Finally, in 1970, a buddy on the force took him along to watch a meet in Los Angeles, and Marv had one of those life-changing encounters that happen along every so often. At the meet his buddy introduced him to another of the competitors, a 6-feet 2-inch 270-pound cop from the city, who looked Marv up and down and then said to the buddy, "You'll never make a lifter out of *this* guy."

As you might imagine, this ate on Marv a bit. The more he brooded the more his ego hurt until finally both he and his ego stood up on their collective hind legs, and allowed as how they

THE PRAYER-LIKE preparation for a heavy deadlift and the frustration of failure.

thought by God they'd do a little power-lifting. And do it they did. That was July of 1970 and by November of that year Marv entered his first contest, a policemen's meet, and totaled an excellent 1,465 at a bodyweight of 193 with lifts of 525 squat, 425 bench press, and 515 deadlift. "I wore tight levis and elbow wraps," Marv told me, "but even so I was mighty proud."

Charged up by this early success, he kept pumping, and soon began to branch out from the policemen's meets to open contests, where he was to meet a man who served for several years as his coach, competitor, and inspiration, Tom Overholtzer. From then on he kept gunning for Tom's records, and in 1973 he finally reached them, passed them, and began to look around for new challenges and training techniques, both of which he found down on the beach at the workout quarters of Bud Ravenscroft, Ernie Steinkirchner, and Terry McCormick. With them, he says he "got serious" and began to study nutrition, to back off a bit from wearing all the heavy wraps, and to lift with his head as well as his body.

In 1974 he was ready to enter national competition, and his debut was all anyone could ask for; he came away from the meet as the national 220-pound champion, having totaled 1,770 via 670 in the squat, 465 in the bench press, and 635 in the deadlift. Later that year, at the World Championships, he upped his total to 1,825, which included a world-record squat of 733.5, but he had the misfortune to be in the same class as the man Marv calls G. L. P.—the Great Larry Pacifico.

In 1975 he was second twice more to G. L. P., both in the Nationals and in the World Championships in Birmingham, England. He did gain a little revenge in early 1976, however, when at a bodyweight of only 221 he made a world-record squat in the 242-pound class with 755, breaking the former record of 752, which had been held by the great Mr. P. He did well again at the World's in 1976, shattering his own 242-pound record with back to back squats of 760 and, on a fourth attempt, 777.5.

Just a few months ago he moved the record up again with *another* back to back series of world marks. After opening with 735, he took 785 for an easy second attempt and new world record, then asked for 810. As he was beginning the lift, the timing buzzer rang, even though it was incorrectly set for two minutes instead of three; so the judges all turned the lift down. Needless to say, Marv was really smoking over the bad call; so he just told the loaders to leave it on and he'd "do the damn thing again." And, with *less* than two minutes rest from the previous 810, he *again* hoisted the weight, which proved to be 806 for his second, or third, world record of the night, depending on your point of view.

He uses the same squat routine now that he's used for the past several years, and anyone would have to agree that Marv would be a fool to tinker with a system which seems to work so ideally. He squats twice each week—Tuesday and Saturday—going light one workout and heavy the next. He cycles his routine so that if he doesn't have a contest coming up soon, he never goes over 405 for five repetitions on Tuesday and never goes over 625 for five on Saturday. You might call this his "coasting" routine. It would be pound for pound as follows:

Tuesday: He begins each workout day with two 220-yard runs (not jogs, not sprints, but *runs*), outside if the weather's good, inside a 200-yard tunnel if it's bad.

135 × as many as he needs to get loose.

135 × 10—On both these first two sets he goes rock bottom, as he wants to really stretch the muscles of the hips,

thighs, and lower back, and he uses a close (14 inches from heel to heel) stance.

225 × 8—Also, with a 14-inch stance, toes pointing out.

315 × 5—Regular stance (never more than 22 inches wide).

405 × 5—Regular stance.

315 × 10 or 12—Back to close stance and rock bottom so as to really pump the thighs and hips full of fresh blood.

Saturday: He begins with the two 220-yard runs.

135 × as many as he needs to get loose.

135 × 10—Deep, as on Tuesday.

225 × 8—Narrow stance, as on Tuesday.

325 × 5—Regular stance from here on up.

425 × 5

525 × 5

625 × 5

315 × 10 or 12—Close stance again, as on Tuesday.

When he knows the date of a forthcoming meet, he backs up 12 weeks from the target date, abandons his "coasting" routine, *in which the poundages stay the same,* and begins his pre-meet cycle. The primary difference between his coasting routine and his pre-meet cycle is that in the cycle he attempts to dramatically increase the amount of weight he handles. His sets and reps stay more or less the same, but he really loads on the iron.

For the first four weeks of his 12-week cycle, he attempts to add five pounds per week so that at the end of the four weeks he'd be handling 425 on Tuesday instead of 405 and 645 on Saturday instead of 625. At this point he begins taking injections of B[12] and upping his vitamin intake (C, E, etc.), and from that point until contest time, he plans to add ten pounds each week for eight weeks. This would bring his last Tuesday workout up to 505 × 5 and his last Saturday workout to 725 × 5. During his final eight weeks, he begins using the 100-pound plates in order to simulate the conditions of a meet; so his poundages would be more or less like this for his final heavy week:

Tuesday: Begins with the two 220-yard runs.
135 × as many as needed to get loose, close stance.
135 × 10—Close stance.
245 × 8—Close stance.
335 × 5—Regular stance from here up.
445 × 5
505 × 5
335 × 10 or 12—Close stance.

Saturday: Begins with his 220-yard runs.
135 × as many as needed to get loose, close stance.
135 × 10—Close stance.
245 × 8—Close stance.
335 × 5—Regular stance from here on up.
445 × 5
535 × 5
645 × 5
725 × 5
335 × 10 or 12—Close stance.

Marvin feels that the light day on Tuesday is just right for him as it keeps both his mind and body sharp. He uses weights that are heavy enough to feed the muscles, but light enough to be no real strain. The heavy-light system seems to keep him from going stale; with it, he's able to train year-round, with no layoffs at all, other than perhaps skipping his set with 425 on the Tuesday after a big meet. He also feels that the program is excellent for helping to build and maintain muscle bulk in the thighs and hips, and a look at the pictures accompanying this chapter should be enough to convince a Missouri mule that where muscular bulk is concerned, Marv knows what he's talking about.

He uses a *relatively* narrow foot spacing for his heavy squats because he feels that with his particular construction it allows him to use his thighs more and to keep his lower back "cocked." He feels that once his mid-back begins to bend he's in real trouble; so he uses a more upright stance than most other powerlifters. Of course in all honesty I have to say that old Marvin is really built for the squat—it's a truly natural lift for him. He makes the heavy ones look light with that jugbutt power of his driving out those sets of five.

He admits that a good part of his success in the squat is due to his structural advantages, but he justifiably points out that the *majority* of his progress has resulted from his willingness to give himself *unsparingly* to his training. "No one," he told me, "works harder than I do." And as hard work so often does, it paid off, as the people out in L. A. were quick to admit the night in March of 1977 when he gave a squatting exhibition at a local meet—the week before the 806 world record—and knocked out five reps with 755, after which he got serious and did *three reps with 800*, weighing about 235. I'm told that seasoned lifters were shocked into literal speechlessness by the performance. After seeing three reps with 800 what *can* you say?

Of course all the hard work in the world wouldn't build the strength for three reps with 800 pounds unless the muscles which were being worked were being nourished and replenished by good food and adequate rest. Like most of the athletes in this book, Marv is careful about his diet, and he watches it year-round. He doesn't care for sweets, but it would be fair to say that he's into beefsteak. He specializes in big steaks, fresh vegetables, cottage cheese, eggs, cheese, fresh fruit, milk, and fruit juices. During the final eight weeks before a meet, in

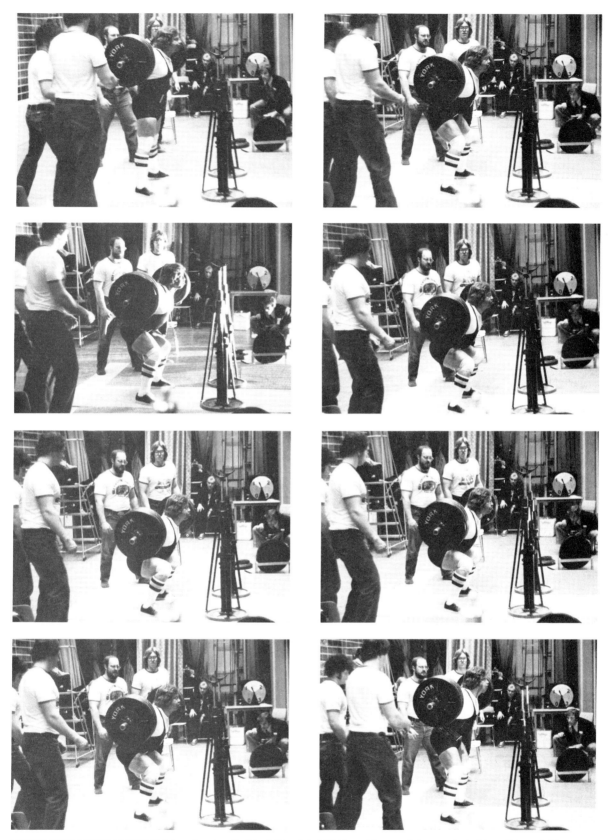

THESE SEQUENCE PHOTOS taken by Jan Todd of Marvin's 777.5 world record demonstrate his solid, upright stance and the good depth he achieves even on the heavy ones. Note the camera flashes which light him up in the third photo in the sequence. Note also that he sticks out his tongue, not a recommended procedure.

order to trim any fat, he cuts out all milk as well as the few beers he sometimes has on the weekend.

His job at the police department requires him to be up before dawn almost every morning; so he has to be extra careful to get enough sleep. He gets off each afternoon at three and trains until six, and by the time he gets home, showers, does his chores (he raises meat animals of various kinds), and eats, he's ready for the sack. In order to be up at 5:30 he turns in on the weekdays no later than

10:30, a sacrifice he's willing to make even as a single man because he knows if he *didn't* bed down early he could kiss his world records goodbye. Of course, Marv's not totally unaware of all the fine-looking women in Southern California; so he reserves the weekends for what he calls "playing and partying."

One of the reasons he trains hard and plays hard is because he *works* hard. Being a patrolman at his own request for 11 years in an area which has the highest per capita crime rate in the U. S. allows

EVEN THOUGH THE deadlift is Marvin's poorest lift, this photo does serve to highlight the incredible thickness and definition of his physique. He looks like he could lift the world if he knew where to take a hold.

for the buildup of more than a little bit of pressure and Marv often ends one of his long days all burned up and frustrated over some bureaucratic hassle or other. "Thank the Lord," he says, "for the weight room. I can go in there and begin to train and feel the poison draining away." He told me this in response to a question I asked him about why he trained—what he got out of it. Besides the calming effect it has after a tough day on the streets, Marv said his training provided a focus to his life, a way of setting goals for himself and then having the pleasure of achieving them. "And more than that," he said, "I love the feeling of being strong—the feeling of superiority. No other words will do. I enjoy being powerful and looking powerful and getting compliments on my lifting and my looks." I guess if we'd admit it, all of us do. "And," he added, "I get off on the moments before, during, and after a big lift when you know you've done your homework and it's time to collect. No feeling can match it."

GOOD FRIENDS AND sometime training partners Doug Young and Marvin Phillips backstage at the 1976 World Championships.

One day, Marv hopes to have some of these moments before, during, and after a 900 squat as a 242-pounder—one of his ultimate goals. He plans to reach it by picking the brains of the best powerlifters in the business. One of the things he likes most about the sport is the cooperation and sharing of information between competitors. I remember seeing him sitting with Pacifico on the plane all the way back from England in 1975 after the World's, picking old G. L. P.'s brain. "They *will* help," Marv insists, "even the great ones, like Larry, if a person will just ask."

He urges all beginners to read all they can find about the sport, but he also thinks they should seek out the most experienced lifters in their area and listen to them as long as they'll talk. He thinks that the most important two weeks of his life were spent in Brownwood, Texas, about a month after the 1976 World Championships. He felt in real need of help with his bench press and his supplements; so he went to his pal Doug Young, the Texas Guru, who was himself glad to get a little help from someone like Marv in the squat. Marv shared his knowledge with Doug, and Doug responded by opening up his own wonderful bag of tricks; so they *both* benefited. "No matter how good you are," Marv said, "you should never be too good to learn something new. I hope to keep learning and keep pushing until I'm the champion of the world in the 220-pound class. And," he said with a smile, "I think I'll do it. Unless, of course, I go out one day on the job and get blown away."

RICKEY CRAIN

Of all the athletes featured in this book, Rickey Crain has the strange distinction of being both the youngest and the one with the most years of experience in the sport of powerlifting. At the age of 24,

he's almost ten years younger than the average age of the rest of the champions I've covered; but he has spent close to ten years more in the iron game than the average time spent in the sport by the other eight people in the book. Sounds impossible, doesn't it? Well, had it not been for one person, it would certainly have been improbable, if not impossible. That one person is his dad, Jack Crain, one of the groundbreakers of powerlifting.

NINE-YEAR-OLD Rickey Crain only weighed 60 pounds but he could pull 135 and was only a year away from triple bodyweight.

Jack took Rickey and his other son Randy to the Oakland Y when they were only three or four years old, and Rickey can't remember a time when he wasn't lifting weights. "I literally grew up on it," he says. "And my earliest memories are of me and Dad and Randy going down to the Y and tossing the weights around." He won his first lifting contest at the age of ten, and that same year he and Randy both made triple bodyweight deadlifts—he with 200 weighing 66 pounds and nine-year-old, 55-pound Randy with 165.

To commemorate this important bit of family history, Rickey's father had two belt buckles made which carried the inscription, Triple Bodyweight. Thinking back on those days, Rickey recalls that his dad used to bribe, threaten, cajole, or shame the boys into being regular in their training, and although Rickey didn't always appreciate it back then, he's mighty glad now that the old man cared enough to use his influence to get them to stick to their programs. "He showed me the way," Rickey told me, "I owe him."

Of course one of the *best* ways to teach is by example. As the Chinese philosopher Lao-tse said, "We teach by what we are," and what Jack Crain was and is is one hell of a lifter. Today, at the age of 50 and at a bodyweight of 165-170, he's *still* improving and can total right at 1,500 pounds with a squat of 500, a bench press of 380 and a deadlift of 620. Naturally this makes his son both proud and confident that his own lifting career will span several more decades. One thing about Rickey is sure—he's off to quite a start.

In the spring of 1977, he established the almost unbelievable world-record total of 1,591 pounds in the lightweight (148.75 pound) class, a total which is the highest pound for pound total ever made, according to the Schwartz formula. And yet as astonishing as this total is, his plans for the next season were to push it even higher. His goal for the 1977 National Championships was 1,700 pounds, made up of a 630 squat, a 390 bench press and a 680 deadlift, and his target for the World Championships two months later in Perth, Australia, was *1,750 pounds* via 650, 400 and 700.

To be honest, I doubt seriously that Rickey will reach these figures; in fact, I doubt if even his *father* expects him to reach them. But that doesn't matter. The important thing—the *crucial* thing—is that *Rickey* believes he'll do it, and this belief energizes his training and gives him the courage to address himself to weights

no man his size has ever lifted. All the lifters in this book, in fact, share this almost obsessive belief in themselves—otherwise, they'd be unable to approach barbells which outweigh them two, three, and even four times. *If the mind won't believe it, the body won't heave it.* Believe it.

THIS IS RICKEY'S lightweight (148.75-pound class) world record, 513.

These stratospheric poundages serve to provide a focus for his pre-contest training cycle by giving him a starting point. Basically, Rickey has four cycles—a six-week cycle, a five-week cycle, a four-week cycle, and a three-week cycle—and he plugs into the appropriate cycle depending on how far ahead the next meet is. For instance, if he had a contest in ten weeks he'd plug into the third week of the five-week cycle, and this would lead him in turn to the four-week cycle and, finally, to the three-week cycle.

What he does in the squat is to predict the poundage he feels he can make on the day of the contest and then take off ten pounds for every week left. In other words, if he plans to squat with 630 on the day of the National meet and the meet is 14 weeks away, he would back off 140 pounds, to 490, and use that as his top single. Then, every week of the 14 pre-meet weeks he would plan to add ten pounds, thus bringing him to the contest date with the gradually built strength to squat with 630.

Being 14 weeks ahead of the meet, he would begin with the fifth week of his six-week cycle. These two weeks (the fifth and sixth weeks of the six-week cycle), plus the five weeks of the five-week cycle, the four weeks of the four-week cycle, and the three of the three-week cycle add up to 14 weeks. The fifth week of his six-week cycle would call for the following sets, reps, and poundages:

THESE PHOTOS SHOW his recent switch from a relatively narrow stance to a wider stance with his toes turned much further out.

Monday
Squat

145 × 10	490 × 1
245 × 6	410 × 8
345 × 4	410 × 8
420 × 1	410 × 8
465 × 1	410 × 8

Pause Squat
390 × 5, with a three second pause at the bottom on each repetition

Wednesday
Squat

145 × 10	420 × 1
245 × 6	465 × 1
345 × 4	490 × 1

Pause Squat
390 × 5, same as Monday

For his three singles (420, 465, and 490), Rickey uses the exact costume that he would wear at a meet—the exact lifting suit, shoes, belt, and knee wraps. Also, he uses the same weight increases between his first and second single and his second and third single that he plans to use at the meet. He always prefers to jump 45 pounds between his first and second attempts and 25 pounds between his second and third. For his four sets of eight on Monday, he drops ten pounds

per repetition from his top single, thus going from 490 to 410. For his set of five in the pause squats, he always drops 100 pounds from his top single of the day. He said quite emphatically when I spoke with him that he considered this final set of pausing squats to be "by far the most important part" of his squatting routine.

After two weeks of the six-week cycle, he's ready for his five-week cycle, which would begin as follows on the first week:

Monday
Squat

145 × 10	520 × 1
245 × 6	470 × 5
345 × 4	470 × 5
450 × 1	470 × 5
485 × 1	470 × 5

Pause Squat
420 × 5

Wednesday
Squat

145 × 10	450 × 1
245 × 6	485 × 1
345 × 4	520 × 1

Pause Squat
420 × 5

As can be seen, the only difference between the six-week cycle and the five-week cycle is that he moves from four sets of eight in the six-week cycle to four sets of five in the five-week cycle. After building up ten pounds per week during each week of the five-week cycle, he's ready to begin the four-week cycle. By then, he'd be up to 570 for a top single; so his first week's workouts would be as follows:

Monday
Squat

145 × 10	570 × 1
245 × 6	520 × 5
345 × 4	530 × 4
445 × 2	540 × 3
500 × 1	550 × 2
545 × 1	560 × 1

Pause Squat
470 × 5

Wednesday
Squat

145 × 10	500 × 1
245 × 6	545 × 1
345 × 4	570 × 1
445 × 2	

Pause Squat
470 × 5

THESE SHOTS DEMONSTRATE the ease with which Rickey is able to reach a legal depth in the squat. Note how high he puts the bar on his neck. Note also that he has turned his belt around so that the wide part is across the front of his body where it provides more leverage.

For his final cycle of three weeks, he would continue adding weight and would train in the following way:

Monday
Squat

145 × 10	600 × 1
245 × 6	570 × 3
345 × 4	580 × 2
445 × 2	590 × 1
520 × 1	580 × 2
575 × 1	570 × 3

Pause Squat
500 × 5

Wednesday
Squat

145 × 10	530 × 1
245 × 6	575 × 1
345 × 4	600 × 1
445 × 2	

By the end of the three-week cycle, he would reach 620 as a top single the week before the meet, and thus be prepared both mentally and physically for his planned competition single with 630 pounds.

As in the squat, Rickey trains his bench twice a week—Tuesdays and Saturdays—but, instead of increasing ten pounds each week, he only looks for a gain of five pounds. Using a 390-pound bench as a contest-day goal, this would mean that he'd drop back to 315 if he were 15 weeks away from the meet. Therefore, his first week's workouts would be as follows:

Tuesday

Bench Press

135 × 10	315 × 1
225 × 5	285 × 3
270 × 3	285 × 3
285 × 1	285 × 3
300 × 1	285 × 3

Pausing Bench Press

240 × 5, with a five-second pause on the chest on each rep

**Narrow-Grip
  Bench Press**

240 × 5	240 × 5

Military Press

135 × 5	175 × 5
175 × 5	175 × 5

Wide-Grip Chin

3 sets of 10

Saturday

Bench Press

same as Tuesday

Pausing Bench Press

same as Tuesday

Military Press

same as Tuesday

Wide-Grip Chin

same as Tuesday

As the contest approaches, rather than switching routines or cycles as he does in the squat, Rickey uses the exact same bench routine—three progressively heavier singles followed by four sets of three—and assistance exercises throughout the final 15 weeks. The only difference—the vital one, naturally—is that he adds five pounds to all his benches every week that he trains. He told me that although he has experimented with many other methods of bench-press training, this one seems to suit him best.

UNDER THE HAWKLIKE eye of judge Peary Rader, young Rickey pulls a big deadlift.

For his deadlift, Rickey divides his final 15 weeks into two equal cycles of seven weeks each and one week (the final one) of complete rest. Projecting a 680 for the forthcoming Nationals, he dropped back to 540 to begin his ascent. His final week of the first seven-week cycle would be as follows:

Friday

**Deadlift
  (sumo style)**

145 × 10	530 × 1
245 × 6	575 × 1
345 × 4	600 × 1
445 × 2	550 × 5

**Deadlift
  (traditional style)**

500 × 5

Deadlift off blocks (traditional stance)—450 × 10, done while standing on blocks which are four or five inches higher than the level of the floor.

For his final seven weeks, he alters the program somewhat, cutting down on his repetitions and gearing for the big singles he'll need at the meet. Assuming he's in the fifth week of his seven-week cycle, his top single would be 650 and his entire workout would be done thus:

Friday
Deadlift
  (sumo style)
145 × 10   580 × 2
245 × 6   625 × 1
345 × 4   650 × 1
445 × 2   620 × 3
545 × 1   620 × 3
Deadlift
  (traditional style)
570 × 3   570 × 3
Deadlift off blocks
  (traditional stance)
520 × 10

Note that throughout the 14 weeks of heavy training he always does his three heavy contest singles in exactly the same way he does his heavy squats. That is he takes them as if he were *in a meet*, wearing competition gear and making the same interattempt weight increases that he intends to use at the meet. As in the squat, he uses a 45-pound jump between

AS HE EXPERIMENTED with different positions, he finally adopted this one *(above)* as ideally suited to his particular body construction. *(Below)* These two shots show him humping over and then flattening his back and preparing to pull.

his first and second attempts and a 25-pound jump between the second and third.

Because of his particular structure (relatively long back and relatively short thighs), Rickey has excellent leverage in the squat. This leverage, plus great strength in his hips and thighs, makes it advantageous for him to use the wide stance, close grip, sumo style in the deadlift. Even though this method of deadlifting allows the bulk of the work to be done by the hips and thighs rather than the back, Rickey realizes that even in the sumo style the back *still* plays a vital role. This realization prompted him to wisely add the traditional style deadlift and the deadlift off blocks to his routine, as these two exercises place more strength-building stress on the muscles of the lower and mid-back than do the sumo-style deadlifts.

In addition to all the exercises already listed, Rickey also does supplementary work for his legs every Monday, Wednesday, and Friday. On Mondays and Wednesdays it follows his squat program, and on Fridays it comes after his deadlifts. He uses the following supplementary exercises three times a week:

Monday, Wednesday, and Friday
Leg Extension
3 moderate sets of 10
Leg Curl
3 moderate sets of 10
Calf Raise
3 moderate sets of 10
Weightless-Calf Raise
2 sets of 50

He never neglects these exercises because he feels they have contributed heavily to his success in the squat. In particular, he thinks the calf raises are absolutely essential for maximum gains. So, taken as a whole, without going back over his poundages, sets and reps, his weekly schedule would look like this:

AT A BODYWEIGHT of just over the middleweight limit, Rickey pulled this 650 deadlift in training in July of 1976.

Monday:
 Squat
 Pause Squat
 Leg Extension
 Leg Curl
 Calf Raise
 Weightless-Calf Raise

Tuesday:
 Bench Press
 Pausing Bench Press
 Narrow-Grip Bench Press
 Military Press
 Wide Grip Chin

Wednesday:
 Squat
 Pause Squat
 Leg Extension
 Leg Curl
 Calf Raise
 Weightless-Calf Raise

Friday:
 Deadlift (sumo style)
 Deadlift (traditional style)
 Deadlift off blocks
 Leg Extension
 Leg Curl
 Calf Raise
 Weightless-Calf Raise

Saturday:
 Bench Press
 Pausing Bench Press
 Narrow-Grip Bench Press
 Military Press
 Chin

In addition, Rickey does 200 sit-ups a day, which tops off what must be one of the most rigorous exercise programs followed by any world-class powerlifter. He seems to thrive on this rather rigid, methodical schedule, but he told me to warn all beginners and intermediates that not only is his routine a very advanced one, it *also* is tailored exactly to his own particular physiological and psychological requirements. Consider yourselves warned.

In order to fuel himself for this high-stress training, he is very careful to concentrate on beef, poultry, fish, eggs, cheese, and fresh fruits and vegetables. As for daily supplements, he takes a good vitamin-mineral tablet, a B complex tablet, energol, and 3000 mg. of vitamin C. Through the years he's tried such things as zinc sulfate, niacin, and ginseng, but he noticed no benefit from them. In the future, he plans to follow his dad's lead and try B^3 and B^7 Complex (hydrosolates), as they are said by some to provide muscle-building assistance similar to anabolic steroids. Besides his nutritious diet, Rickey keeps close tabs on his energy level so that he knows when he needs a little extra sacktime.

All this good food and rest have been put to good use, as a glance at the accompanying photos will confirm. Besides his huge, wide-swept thighs, take note of the fact that in the squat his lifting belt is turned so that the wide part is on the front of his body. Many lifters, including Rickey, have noticed that not only do they get more abdominal support this way, but they *also* get a rebound effect when the belt provides a brace between the hip joint and the lower part of the rib cage. In order for this to work best, the belt should be pushed fairly low on the hips and it should be pulled as tightly as it can possibly be pulled. Anyone having a belt made could save themselves the trouble of turning it around simply by having it made the maximum allowable width (10 centimeters) all the way around. Marvin Phillips and his father make belts this way, and they're the best I've ever seen.

Within the last couple of years, Rickey has learned other tricks of the trade besides turning his belt around, such as placing his feet wide enough and turning his toes out enough so that the large, powerful muscles of the hips and the rear of the thighs are brought into full play. Also, since his Achilles tendons are sufficiently loose for him to be able to "break parallel" without using shoes with high heels, he has sensibly chosen to squat in low-heeled, but solid, tennis shoes. As the pictures show, he places the bar extraordinarily high on the trapezius muscles of his neck, which forces him to maintain a very upright position throughout the lift. This position is dictated by his particular body type—for him it is ideal, allowing him to go below parallel without reaching a particularly acute angle at the knee. Using this upright style, he "sits" into the squat, dips just below parallel, and before you know it, he's got another world record.

Most of Rickey's career has been one success after another, but last year at the 1976 World Championships he had a meet I'm sure he'd much rather forget.

After easily winning the Nationals, he made the mistake of allowing his training bodyweight to creep up far too high, all the way into the 170-pound range. This, plus a poorly planned pre-contest reducing schedule, left him a pound or two too heavy when the time limit ran out for the 148.75 pound weigh-in. Even with steambaths, last minute starvation, and diuret-ics he was *still* unable to make it, and this failure contributed significantly to America's loss to Great Britain in the team championship. I doubt that I'll ever forget how Rickey looked as he sat naked on the toilet only minutes before the weigh-in time was up. Elbows on his knees, head in his hands as if in prayer, he was the quintessence of dejection. Coincidentally, I had used that same toilet earlier in the day and had chuckled at the old but now ironically timely men's room standby.

> Here I sit, broken-hearted
> Tried to——but only——

A lesser man than Rickey would no doubt have simply enlisted in the French Foreign Legion and disappeared after such a disgrace, but he swallowed his pride, got back in shape, and set the lifting world on its ear with that monumental 1,591 pound total. Perhaps he was sustained during his tribulations by his devout faith in Christ. He was then and is now a student at the Southwest Baptist Theological Seminary, where he plans to get a master's degree and, finally, a Ph. D. degree in religious education. Eventually, he hopes to teach or do youth work at a church. Hopefully, he'll stay in powerlifting, because with his youth and strength and consistent family support, he could become one of the legends of the game.

IN 1977, AT a bodyweight of 275, Doug Young worked on up from this warmup with 315 to his first official 600-pound bench press.

chapter 3

THE BENCH PRESS

Among the largest and most impressive of the muscles of the upper body are the pectorals, the deltoids, and the triceps. All three develop quickly, and all three are given a full and thorough workout by the bench press, far and away the most popular upper-body exercise among athletes, bodybuilders, fitness buffs and, of course, powerlifters. Whether its popularity derives from its wonderful developmental qualities, from the fact that it's one of the physically easiest and most pleasant of exercises or, more likely, from both, it can be safely said that as long as there are barbells there will be bench presses.

This was not always the case. In the last part of the 19th and first part of the 20th centuries—surely the heyday of professional strongmen—the press on bench or supine press was almost nonexistent.

Other than "belly toss" specialists such as the Russian George Lurich, who would lie on his back on the floor, hold a barbell in his hands, lower it and then "toss" it back up from his abdomen by pushing upward with his legs as his hips came more than a foot off the floor, virtually no one else ever did the lift. In a way, the bench press could then be said not to have been *invented* yet. It was actually not until during and after World War II that the lift came well and truly into its own. Once benches were widely available and people got to experience the natural high that comes from the type of terminal pump that only the bench press can give you, however, there was no question that it was a lift whose time had come.

If I were to pick two men who had the most to do with spreading the word about the bench press, they would be Marvin

Eder, the marvelously built 200-pounder, who was the strongest man of his weight in the world in the early and middle 1950s; and Doug Hepburn, the Canadian Superheavyweight World Olympic Lifting Champion, who was almost certainly the first man to legitimately bench press 500 pounds. Both of these men captured the imagination of the lifting world with their great strength and upper body size; they are the giants on whose shoulders stood those of us who came later. Because of the great popularity of the lift, there was never any real question that it would be included once the powerlifts became organized. The current IPF rules for the performance of the lift are listed below.

CANADA'S DOUG HEPBURN, who back in the 1950's became the first man ever to reach 500 pounds in the bench press, sported a pair of arms that must have been well over 20 inches around.

Bench Press
1. The lifter may elect to assume one of the following two positions on the bench, which must be maintained during the lift: (a) with head, trunk, and legs extended on the bench, knees locked, heels on a second bench; or (b) with head, trunk (including buttocks) extended on the bench, feet flat on the floor.

2. The referee's signal shall be given when the bar is absolutely motionless at the chest.
3. After the referee's signal, the bar is pressed vertically to straight arms length and held motionless for the referee's signal to replace the bar.
4. The width of the bench shall not be less than 25 cm., or more than 30 cm. The height shall not be less than 35 cm., and not more than 45 cm. The length shall not be less than 1 meter 22 cm. and shall be flat and level.
5. The spacing of the hands shall not exceed 81 cm. measured between the forefingers.
6. If the lifter's costume and the bench top are not of a sufficient color contrast to enable the officials to detect a possible raising of the buttocks, the bench top shall be covered accordingly.
7. In this lift the referees shall station themselves at the best points of vantage.
8. For those lifters who elect to use position (b) and whose feet do not touch the floor, the platform may be built up to provide firm footing.
9. A maximum of four and a minimum of two spotter-loaders shall be mandatory; however the lifter may enlist one or more of the official spotter-loaders to assist him in removing the bar from the racks.

Causes for Disqualification for the Bench Press
1. During the uplifting, any change of the elected lifting position.
2. Any raising or shifting of the lifter's head, shoulders, buttocks, or legs from the bench, or movement of the feet.
3. Any heaving or bouncing of the bar from the chest.

4. Allowing the bar to sink excessively into the lifter's chest prior to the uplift.

5. Any uneven extension of the arms.

6. Stopping of the bar during the press proper.

7. Any touching of the bar by the spotters, before the referee's signal to replace the bar.

8. Failure to wait for the referee's signal.

9. Touching against the uprights of the bench with the feet.

10. Touching the shoulders against the uprights of the bench.

11. Allowing the bar to touch the uprights of the bench during the lift.

DOUG YOUNG

Once upon a time there was a young athlete of unusual ability. He played football during high school and college and started every game he was well enough to start. But, like so many other young men, his knees just couldn't stand the strain, and so his desire to play pro ball was sublimated as he eased into marriage and a career. The tight, rugged sinews of his playing days began to go slack as he lived the life of a middle-class American—eating too much, drinking too much, tubing it too much, and sitting too much on his fat aspirations. His weight grew to 240 pounds, and he was teased about his size by the men with whom he worked. And so, on a bet with these men, he began to diet, he began to lose and, in less than two months, he stepped on the scales of the local gym and weighed 178 pounds. That same day, to test his strength, he worked up in the bench press to a maximum single of 305 pounds. That was on January 26, 1973. Approximately eight months later, on October 1, 1973, he came back into the gym, weighed in at

260 and worked up in the bench to a high of 540 pounds. Yes—540 pounds—a gain of 235 pounds in eight months. These truly incredible gains were made by Doug Young, a man who is now the 242-pound champion of the world.

In late 1973, I had been hearing rumors of Doug's lifting from friends in Texas, and so on a trip to Austin over the holiday season, I arranged for him to come down from his home in Brownwood so I could see this wonder of nature for myself. Actually, I had met Doug years before while he was playing ball for Texas Tech, and I knew of his natural ability in the bench press. But I had never seen him train.

He came into the Texas Athletic Club on the day of our prearranged workout and he was quite a sight. He stands about 5 feet 11 inches, and he carries most of his 245 pounds from his waist up. Some men are broad, some are thick, but very few are both. Big Doug is one of the few. Dressed in tight Levi's, a short-sleeved shirt, and cowboy boots, he looked strong enough to bulldog a buffalo.

DOUG YOUNG, PULLING with the most impressive set of muscles in powerlifting, locks out a heavy deadlift and wins his second world title.

The word had gotten around to all the local horses, and so we had a big bunch at the T. A. C. when Doug began to train. No one, however, except Ivan Putski, the Polish pro-wrestler, seemed very interested in benching that day; and we suspect that Putski didn't know, or care, what was on the bar. The rest of us, though, surely knew—and cared. Doug took 135 for 10 reps as a warm-up and then went on to get singles with 225, 315, 405, 485, 505, and 520. He then dropped back to 405 for eight repetitions and 315 for 15. Not bad seeing as how he had just lost weight down from 260 in an effort to stay somewhere near the 242-pound class limit.

I had a fine time that day watching Doug and talking with the wonderful old rowdies down at the T. A. C., enough to make me want to hit the comeback trail. (If only it wouldn't hit back.) During the course of that day's lifting, I got some of the details of Doug's meteoric gains in the bench press and in muscular bodyweight, and I want to begin with this information.

Doug kept records of his progress in the bench, and he breaks it down this way. During his first 42 workouts, he gained 42 pounds of bodyweight (hitting 220) and 160 pounds in the bench press (reaching 465). The next 42 workouts saw him adding 40 more pounds of bodyweight (to 260) and 75 pounds of bench pressing strength (to 540).

Throughout this eight-month period, Doug concentrated almost entirely on the bench press and the upper body. His workouts were constant during the entire time. They consisted of the following exercises with the weights listed being the heaviest he handled during that period:

Bench Press

135 × 12	500 × 1	425 × 1	540 × 1
225 × 6	515 × 1	465 × 1	490 × 9
325 × 2	530 × 1	485 × 1	300 × 14
375 × 2	540 × 1		

Williams-Front Deltoid Raise
50 pounds for 3 sets of 15
Triceps Press
175 pounds for 6 sets of 6
Stiff-Arm Pulldown on Lat Machine
100 pounds for 6 sets of 6
Flys with Cables
50 pounds for 6 sets of 6
One-Arm Concentration Curl
55 pounds for 6 sets of 6
One-Arm Rowing Motion
110 pounds for 6 sets of 6

Doug did this same workout three days a week (Monday, Wednesday, and Friday) throughout this eight-month period, varying it only by going for heavy doubles in the bench instead of singles if he happened to be sore. The only leg and back work he did was four or five singles in the squat every ten days, and six or seven singles in the deadlift every 15 days. This concentrated upper-body work brought his arm measurement to 19.75 inches and his chest to a full 60 inches. That day, at 245, he said his chest had dropped to 55 inches. If the 60-inch measurement was accurately taken, it is the largest on record for a man of his weight.

In 1974 he continued to train, hoping to win the National Championships, but his plans were thwarted by the return to lifting of John Kuc, former World Superheavyweight Champion, who reduced to the 242-pound class and beat Doug out of first place with a spectacular 815 deadlift. At that point, a lesser man than Doug would have given up, gone home, popped the top on a cold Coors, and retired in front of the TV set; but Doug simply went back to Texas, drew up a new routine, and decided that 1975 would be his year, John Kuc or no John Kuc. And so with an eye on the 1975 Nationals, Doug

THESE SEQUENCE SHOTS are of Doug's tremendous 562.5 at last year's world championships.

began to hit it, working a little harder than before on his squat and deadlift but still concentrating on his old standby, the bench press.

The 1975 Nationals were held that year in York, Pennsylvania, and lifters from all over the country were staying at the Yorktowne, a fine old hotel in the downtown section. My wife and I had also booked a room there, mainly to visit with old friends, but also to be handy to the marvelous bounty of the Yorktowne's Friday night seafood buffet. When we checked in I learned at the desk that Doug had arrived earlier in the afternoon, and so when we got to our room, I called him and we arranged to meet that evening to feast on the buffet and catch up on old times.

Jan and I got there first and made a run through the boiled shrimp and fresh crabmeat. We had just settled down at my preferred corner table to enjoy a long evening of good food when two things happened that made an impression on me—I don't suppose I'll ever forget them. The first thing that happened was that Doug Young walked a foot or two past the big double doors of the dining room and just stood there—his shoulders seeming to touch each doorjamb and his deeply tanned 22-inch neck slowly turning this way and that as he looked for us in the crowd. But the *second* thing, the *important* thing, was that when Doug walked into the room, the entire room grew quiet. Everyone, lifters and nonlifters, stopped talking, stopped eating, and simply stared at what they knew was one of the most astounding creatures on God's earth. Doug was wearing tight Levi's again, along with a cowboy shirt and a pair of handmade western boots, and let me tell you he was a showstopper.

Anyone who can take the minds of 200 people off of heaping platefuls of some of the best food in the world has got to really be something. And Doug is. I've seen most of the top bodybuilders of the last 20 years and all of the top lifters, but in casual street clothes the most impressive physical specimen of all—bar none—is the big studhorse from Texas who silenced that huge roomful of hungry people with the slim-hipped, bull-shouldered, dangerous-looking splendor of his awesome physical presence.

He had gotten thicker in the upper body, trimmer in the waist, and harder all over in the year since I'd seen him; and I could tell by the look on his face as he sat down at our table with a plateful of lobster that he came to York to win. And win he did, easily outdistancing his nearest opponent and earning a spot on the U.S. team for the World Championships to be held that November in Birmingham, England. As the meet was the first time the World's was being held outside the U.S., I decided to attend, and so I got to watch Doug fulfill the promise I knew he had when I wrote in an article in 1974:

Doug is a rarity—a naturally strong, competitive man who has the capacity to push himself toward a distant, financially unrewarding goal. Steve Stanko was such a man, as were

DESPERADOS WAITING FOR a train—left to right: Robert Young, Terry Todd, Ivan Putski, Doug Young, Jesse Wood, Bob Boothe, and R.L. "Philippine" Moos. *(Right)* Wood and Todd spot Doug as he comes up from a training squat of 500 pounds.

John Davis, Gary Gubner, and Ken Patera. If Doug is able to avoid injuries and maintain his enthusiasm, he has the capacity to join the select ranks of those men listed above. He could well become the strongest man at his bodyweight in the world.

Doug was far better than the second-best man in the world in 1975, and he continued his dominance throughout 1976, defeating the overrated Jon Cole at the Nationals in Arlington, Texas. Cole came to Arlington and put out the word that he'd never been beaten and never planned to be. But after the squat was finished he was so far behind Doug that he was scared into starting too high in the bench press, and so he bombed out of the meet by failing to get credit for any of his three bench-press attempts. Meanwhile,

old Doug just waited backstage till all the commotion was over, then asked the loaders to add 50 pounds to what Cole failed with and went out and shoved it overhead with all the controlled fire of which a true champion is capable.

He went on to defend his World Championship in York, scoring a 2,000 pound total, easily outdistancing his opposition and tying 360-pound Don Reinhoudt in the bench press by making a powerful third attempt with 562.5 pounds. As this is being written, Doug has gone back to his usual training weight of 250 to 255 pounds after having gone to 275 in March of 1977 in order to take a crack at the world superheavyweight bench press record (the record is 610 pounds and is held by Wayne Bouvier, Jim Williams' 675 having been made before world records became official). Unfortunately, Doug

IN THE SPRING of 1977, a reunion of sorts was held at the Texas Athletic Club in Austin, Texas and some of the folks who showed up were, from left to right, Jack Fritsch, one of the strongest-handed men of all time; Doug Young; Jan Todd; Bob Young, and Terry Todd.

tore a pectoral muscle just before the contest and was "only" able to bench a measly 600 pounds. Poor little thing.

The question is—now that we know the full extent of his strength—how did he get that way? Since that early spurt of strength described earlier in this chapter, Doug has considerably refined his bench press routines until now he has a program which seems to him ideal for his particular psychophysiological makeup. When he is specializing on the bench press, which is most of the time, he uses the following sets, repetitions, and weights, and he does this program *every other day:* Monday, Wednesday, Friday, Sunday, Tuesday, etc.

Bench Press
  (32-inch grip)

135 × 10	455 × 2
225 × 8	500 × 2
315 × 6	550 × 2
405 × 2	570 × 1

Bench Press
  (22-inch grip)
405 × 10

Bench Press
  (36-inch grip)
380 × 10

Triceps Press
225 × 6, 4 sets

COLLECTION TIME FOR all that hard work. Bob Hoffman has just presented the trophies for the 1976 World Championships to Saarelainen of Finland, 2nd; Young of the U.S., 1st; and Phillips of the U.S., 3rd.

When Doug reaches the above poundages, he figures that he's good for a 580 second attempt in competition. He feels that the above routine is excellent for reaching a maximum single in the bench press, but he considers it a poor way to gain the sort of bulk and strength which is usually trained for in the off-season. For maximum strength and bulk, Doug recommends the following system as he says it builds muscle and power without burning you out. He uses the program twice each week, with the following approximate poundages:

Bench Press
  (32-inch grip)

135 × 10	470 × 6
225 × 8	470 × 6
315 × 6	470 × 6
405 × 3	470 × 6
450 × 2	

On the last set he does as many reps as he can, adding five pounds to his basic workout weight for each extra repetition over six. For example, if he got eight reps on his last set with 470, he'd use 480 for his four heavy sets in his following workout.

Triceps Press
225 × 6, 4 sets

Another Young routine is the one he uses during the weeks before a contest when he plans to go for a big total (rather than just for a record bench press). During the first three weeks of this program, he alternates the bulk and power routine listed above with the following sets, reps, and weights. He does each of these programs once per week.

Bench Press
  (32-inch grip)

135 × 10	530 × 3
225 × 8	530 × 3
315 × 6	530 × 3

405 × 2   530 × 3
455 × 2   530 × 3
500 × 2

**Bench Press
  (22-inch grip)**
405 × 10

**Bench Press
  (36-inch grip)**
380 × 10

Triceps Press
225 × 6, 4 sets

The above poundages are figured on the basis of a top weight in his alternate program of four heavy sets of six with 480 pounds. He attempts to keep his five sets of three about 50 pounds higher than his four sets of six.

ANOTHER SHOT OF the 700-plus deadlift with which Doug successfully defended his world title.

For his last five workouts before a big meet, he uses the five-sets-of-three program for the first three sessions and then cuts back on his reps so that in his final two workouts he does five heavy sets of two repetitions. These last two workouts would be done as follows:

**Bench Press
  (32-inch grip)**
135 × 10   550 × 2
225 × 8   550 × 2
315 × 6   550 × 2
405 × 2   550 × 2
455 × 2   550 × 2
500 × 2

On this last set he would try to get three reps, or even four, if possible.

This last training session would be on Tuesday or Wednesday if the contest was to be held on Saturday. During the time Doug is using this six-week cycle, he will also be doing his very limited workouts in the squat and deadlift. When I asked him how he trained now that he was "serious" about the total, he smiled and said, "Terry, I could bs you and give you a fancy squat and deadlift program, but you and I would both know it was a lie; so I'll just give you the barebones truth. When I'm on my six-week pre-contest cycle I squat and deadlift only once each eight days, using a 5, 4, 3, 2, 1 program, with 25-pound jumps between sets."

ONE OF THE broadest-shouldered men of any weight anywhere, Doug is caught by the camera of Doug White in the hotel as he waits to leave for the competition.

The following workouts are the ones he said were the best he'd ever made in training. His bodyweight was about 255 at the time.

Squat

225 × 10	625 × 4
315 × 5	650 × 3
425 × 5	675 × 2
525 × 5	700 × 1
600 × 5	

Deadlift
(no straps on these sets)

405 × 5	670 × 5
550 × 5	695 × 4

Deadlift
(from here on up use straps to save hands)

720 × 3	770 × 1
745 × 2	

His all-time bests, both witnessed by dozens of people in a heavy workout one day at the Texas Athletic Club in Austin, are 715 × 2 in the squat, 755 × 4 (almost five), and 805 × 1 in the deadlift. Those of us who know him realize that he hasn't even begun to realize his potential in the squat and the deadlift, mainly because he trains them so infrequently. We all hope he'll buckle down to a heavy schedule for a year or so one of these days and move the 242-pound records clear out of sight, though we realize that it might be impossible for him to keep his weight within the limit if he really worked hard on his hips, legs, and lower back. Perhaps we'll have to wait until the 275-pound class is formally introduced before Doug shows us what he can do if he really tries.

As it is, Doug has all he can do to keep his weight within a reasonable distance of the 242-pound class limit. He carries no extra flesh, as a casual glance at the accompanying photos will reveal. He lives on a diet 90 percent of which consists of tuna fish, cottage cheese, and yogurt in order to keep his weight from creeping

upward. The other 10 percent is made up of various kinds of meat and salads. He also takes liquid protein, but the only vitamin pills he takes are vitamin C (1,000 mg. per day, hardly a large amount). He recommends that beginners pay strict attention to their diet and that they spend their first year or so specializing on four or five sets of midrange repetitions (four to six) in the three powerlifts.

Although Doug's diet obviously influences his physique, a great deal of his unusually impressive appearance is a result of certain natural advantages, such as the previously mentioned narrow hips and his almost freakish shoulder-bone width. These advantages, plus rather trim joints and an obviously wonderful metabolism, account for much of the speed with which his body adapts—through muscle mass and strength—to the stress of his exercise program.

FREQUENTLY BOTHERED BY cramps, Doug gets his back loosened up before benching an official 600.

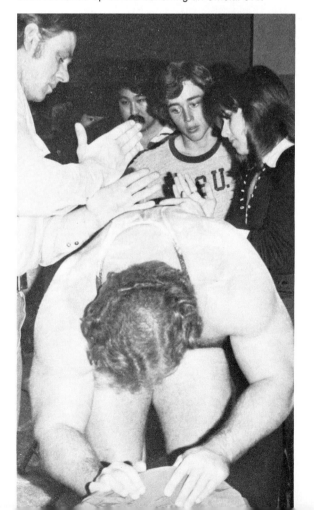

And possibly, just possibly, there is *another* reason for his phenomenal strength and muscular development, a reason which has to do with the *way* Doug does his bench presses. In all my years of watching people train and compete, I have never seen anyone do benches the way Doug does them. The *difference* between Doug and other benchers is the *slowness* with which he lowers the bar to his chest. Whether there is 60 pounds on the bar or 600, Doug lets it down *slow*, people, *slow*, perhaps taking as long as five seconds from the top position until the bar touches his chest. You have to see it to believe it.

I've asked him about it several times and the reason he gives has nothing to do with bodybuilding, but with *positioning*. He says that in order to get a maximum explosion off the chest it's necessary to have the bar in the perfect spot on the chest, and that there's no better way to insure this exact position than to lower the bar gently into the absolute middle of this "power point." *My* hunch is that besides helping Doug in the performance of the lift either physically or psychologically or both, this extreme slowness has had more than a little to do with both his strength and his eye-popping, button-popping development. Recent strength research seems to indicate (not unanimously but in a majority of cases) that *eccentric contraction* (going backwards through the normal range of movement for a muscle, letting the bar down in the bench press rather than pushing it up, in other words) builds strength faster than either *concentric contraction* (pushing the bar up, for example) or *isometric contraction*, (pushing against a bar which *won't* move).

Of course I may be wrong about this, but I somehow doubt it. He's damn sure doing *something* right, as his measurements indicate. At a bodyweight of 242,

his neck is 22 inches, his thighs are 29 inches, and his upper arms are 20 inches; but at 275 they jump to 23.5 inches, 30 inches, and 21.25 inches respectively.

Many people who see Doug for the first time and who are familiar with the iron game wonder why he doesn't go into bodybuilding since there is now a little money to be made by the top men. I asked Doug about this, and he said that although he had great respect for the leading bodybuilders, he had no plans to switch sports, adding the interesting comment that he thought the relationship between a bodybuilder and a lifter was very much the same as that between a quarterback and a linebacker in football. He went on to say that certain personality traits were characteristic of linebackers and that he considered himself more the linebacker (lifter) type than the quarterback (bodybuilder) type.

Doug does know his football, by the way. He was All-State and All-American in high school, and was on his way to college stardom when knee injuries ended his career. Even though he played only seven games in his best year in college, he still was only one vote away from winning the lineman of the year award in the Southwest Conference. His interest in the game is still keen, mainly because his older and bigger (6-feet 2-inch, 275 pounds) brother Bob is a starting offensive guard for the St. Louis Cardinals. Bob has played pro ball for 12 or 13 years now and in the past three years he has developed into the strongest man—by far—in the game as a result of his off-season workouts with Doug. Of all the many men I have known in my life, Bob has the greatest natural gift of strength, but for years he played pro ball—almost always in the starting lineup—without the benefit of weight training. He gives Doug credit for rejuvenating his fading career, and he pays back the favor by being

Doug's main training partner in the off-season and his main supporter all year long.

Of course another of Doug's main supporters is his beautiful, diminutive wife, Bev, who puts up with a lot to keep the big man happy. Doug and Bev have two fine boys—Payton, who is seven, and Brandon, who is five. Doug has a good job with the railroad and he also runs a heavy-duty lifting gym when he's at home in Brownwood, mainly just to have a good place to train. One of Doug's goals is to bench 600 as a 242-pounder, but his biggest hope is that the 275-pound class becomes official. It is as a 275-pounder that he feels he could realize his fullest potential, and I agree with him. He feels that after a year or two of adjusting to and training at the 275-pound limit he could reach a squat of 850, a bench press of 640 to 675, and a deadlift of 850. If

HOW CAN A 5 foot 11 inch man weigh 275 and still look so trim? Only Doug knows, and the big stud's not talking.

anything, I think his predictions are conservative. I suspect he could deadlift 900 pounds at a bodyweight of 275 if he trained for it and if his hands would stand the strain. Eventually, he plans to let his bodyweight slide up to 300 or more for an assault on the barrier bench press of 700 pounds, a weight previously thought to be attainable only by bull gorillas, Kodiak bears, and Jim Williams. Well, look out all you animals, yonder comes the studhorse.

MIKE MacDONALD

Throughout my many years of training for, competing in, and reporting on powerlifting, I've seen many feats of strength which were extraordinary, even unbelievable. I remember one hot afternoon down at the Texas Athletic Club in Austin when a friend of mine, Jack Fritsch, tightened the jaws of the hard-to-shock troops who were training there when he placed a pair of the old-time, thick York 45-pound plates up on their rims with the smooth sides out and then reached down with one hand and pinch-gripped them up to his knees. Unbelievable.

And how could I forget the first time I saw Paul Anderson in the more-than-adequate flesh? It was at an exhibition in Dallas following a contest, and since I'd been competing, I'd been unable to watch him warm up backstage. Thus my first view of him was as he rounded the corner from backstage, stopped to chalk his hands, then walked purposefully to the 400-pound barbell. The world record in the press at that time was around 420, and though I knew Paul had done more, I still expected that he would have to hump a little to handle so awesome a weight. I was simply not prepared to see even the legendary Paul Anderson clean and press 400 pounds like it was made of papier-mache instead of pig iron. It was unbelievable.

But of all the things I've ever seen which were hard to believe, perhaps none strains the limits of the mind quite like Mike MacDonald's bench pressing. I have seen men who were stronger on the bench, such as Big Jim Williams, who came within about one RCH of locking out 700 one year at the World Championships; and I have seen stricter benchers, such as Ronnie Ray, the former 181- and

HOW IS IT possible for these arms to bench press over 600 pounds?

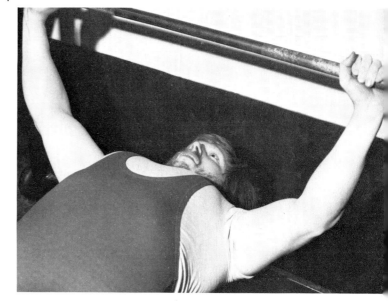

198-pound record holder who used to train for the bench by holding the bar on his chest for 30 seconds (often with over 400 pounds) before pressing it. But never have I come even *close* to seeing a man who was so strong, so strict, and yet so small in the arms and shoulders as Mike MacDonald.

The one thing that really separates powerlifters from Olympic lifters in terms of how their bodies look is the huge arm-shoulder-chest development of the power-lifter. The top guns in the bench—with virtually no exceptions—are extremely heavy and muscular in the deltoids, triceps, biceps, pectorals, and lats (the spreading muscles under the arms which give the back a V shape); and almost always their upper arms and forearms are very thick, giving the impression of a massive tree limb from wrist to shoulder.

Whether these men are able to bench press such colossal weights because of their enormous upper body musculature or whether they develop the musculature as a result of pressing the weights is a question that Mike MacDonald doesn't even *try* to answer. Mike doesn't particularly worry about arm size; he just keeps on using those frail wrists and relatively slender arms to create world record after world record after world record to the utter *astonishment* of lifting fans everywhere.

When Big Jim Williams got ready to bench you *expected* the weights to obey. After all, what choice did they have when faced by an upper body that looked like a brown nylon sack full of bowling balls? Likewise, when Doug Young walks out to bench, the judges take one look at him and begin to signal "good lift" before he even touches the bar. Not so with old Mike. Only death or coma could erase from my mind the memory of the first time I saw him lift. It was in late 1973 at the World Powerlifting Championships in

Harrisburg, Pennsylvania. He had reduced his weight to the lightheavyweight (181.75 pound) class in an attempt to break the world record, and I was very anxious to see him lift as I had heard so much about him.

I remember thinking as he came out for his world record attempt at 470 pounds that there was simply *no way* for someone with arms and shoulders like his to bench press almost 300 pounds over his own bodyweight. I remember watching as he walked quietly out, eased back down onto the bench, unracked the 470, lowered it slowly and deliberately to his chest and then, *wonder of wonders*, drove it to arms' length with the power of a hydraulic carjack. You have to keep in mind that the photos accompanying this article were taken very recently; they show Mike weighing around 230 pounds; so simply deduct 50 pounds with your mind's eye and you'll see what I saw that night in Harrisburg when I got my first look at the man who was then, is now, and will perhaps always be the greatest pound-for-pound bench presser in the world.

Mike got his start at the age of 17 when he began training with friends. Always naturally strong, he bench pressed 320 pounds at a bodyweight of 170 in the state meet after only four months on the weights. At that time Mike's small-boned frame was 5-feet 9-inches tall and it included a pair of 14.5 inch arms; so you can imagine the amazement he caused at that first contest. Bitten hard by the iron bug, he continued to train and compete and within two years he made an official 405 bench press at a 178-pound bodyweight.

Then, in 1968, facing the draft, he joined the Navy and many of his gains were drained away through what seemed to Mike like endless hours of group calisthenics. He recalls with a mixture of distaste and pride one hot afternoon in basic training when his 6-feet 4-inch, 225-pound drill instructor decided to show the recruits how to do push-ups. Mike says that the big DI seemed to always be looking for ways to make the young men feel weak and stupid, and that the push-up exhibition was obviously set up for the same reason.

MIKE'S STYLE IS a straightforward one—no tricks or exaggerated bridge.

And sure enough, after a long talk about what sissified wimps they were, the DI knocked out 60 or 70 push-ups and then ordered his men, one by one, to see how close they could come to matching him. As first one and then another failed, a plan began to form in Mike's mind and so when his turn came he had one of his buddies climb onto his back and then he proceeded to knock out 20 push-ups, after which he turned to the DI and said, "Now try that." Of course he caught, as he says, "a good deal of hell" for it, but he admits to feeling it was worth it.

Shortly after finishing his basic training, he was sent for a year to Vietnam, and he says he passed the long nights in

the bush by dreaming that one day he would follow the lead of his hero Ronnie Ray and create world records in the bench press when his life returned to normal. Happily, this wasn't long in coming, and he spent his final year in the service stationed in Minneapolis, where he had good training facilities and such workout partners as Ken Patera, the giant American Olympic lifter and all-around strongman.

Under these conditions his bench press and his bodyweight both shot up, and within a year he had brought his bench up from a post-Vietnam 230 to an official 480, weighing 215. The next year he entered the Junior National Powerlifting Championships (open to anyone who has won neither the Seniors or the Juniors) and not only made a new Junior National Record in the bench press with 539, but also squatted 655, and deadlifted 640 to total 1,835 and win the Best Lifter trophy. These lifts demonstrate what Mike can do in the squat and deadlift if he trains on them, which he rarely does, preferring instead to specialize in the bench.

In 1973, he trained down to the light-heavyweight class again and set an American record (world records not yet being official) of 484.75. Following the 484.75, he made a 470 official world record (which I described earlier) at the 1973 World Championships, a record which still stands as this is being written. The following year Mike went up to the middleheavyweight (198.75 pound) class, and at the state meet in Minnesota he shattered the world bench-press record twice by lifting 535 and 540 back to back, yet these two great lifts were never official because there were no high-ranking card-holders present to "pass" the lifts (see the appendix for details on the rules).

Mike then moved up into the newly formed 220.5-pound class and broke his friendly archrival Larry Pacifico's world record in the bench by making 555.75. Later that year he and Larry met head to head in the 1974 World Championships in York, Pennsylvania, and when the chalk dust settled, Larry had driven Mike to another world record in the 220's, this time with 573.25, which as of June 1977 was still the record. The 573.25 is not, however, Mike's best official effort in this class because early in 1975 he hoisted 585 in a contest in North Dakota only to lose the lift as a world record because of the aforementioned problem of cardholders.

In 1975, Mike made a judgmental error by driving 1,300 miles almost straight through the day of the National Championships. He was so fatigued that he did far less than his best and was outbenched by the powerful Pacifico. Stung by the defeat, Mike dropped again into the 198.75-pound class and added another bodyweight class to his list of world rec-

ords with a bench of 523.5. Pacifico, however, had ideas of his own about records, and he upped the mark to 529.5 and then published a challenge to Mike saying, in effect, "You won in 1974, I won in 1975, so let's have it out for the title in 1976 in the 198-pound class at the National Championships."

And at the Nationals they met, along with a powerfully built Californian, Bud Ravenscroft, and the three of them provided the greatest display of bench pressing ever seen in the middle-heavyweight class. Even though Larry "only" reached 505 for a second attempt, and Bud made "only" his opener with 500, it was still the only time that three men in so light a bodyweight class had all made 500 pounds. As for our boy Mike, he really smoked them, ending up with an easy, solid 540 for another world record (actual weight: 539.75). From that day in August

MIKE PREPARES HIS mind for an assault on a 615 bench press.

of 1976 until now, Mike has held the world record in four different body-weight classes: 181.75, (470 pounds); 198.25 (539.75 pounds); 220.5 (573.25 pounds); and 242.5 (577 pounds), surely one of the most amazing records in the history of sport.

Perhaps now would be as good a time as any to examine the techniques and the routines this phenomenon has used to reach and dominate the bench press. I should start by making a point which ought to be obvious, which is that *only by specializing in the bench press* has Mike been able to be so successful in raising and lowering his bodyweight while maintaining world-class strength. Don't misunderstand me. Mike would be a threat to the world record in several classes in the bench even if he were to train as hard on the squat and deadlift as he does on his beloved press, but he would not be quite as good as he is now in jumping from class to class and creating records in four or five bodyweight divisions. I say "four or five" because it is Mike's intention to

THIS UNUSUAL PHOTO, taken directly above Mike as he drives out of a heavy bench press, shows the positions of his arms and shoulders relative to the bar.

one day soon hold the world mark in the superheavyweight (unlimited) class, and as the official world record in that class stands at 610 as this is being written (Jim Williams' 675 having been made prior to the time when world records became "official"), Mike should be able to do it as he gave an exhibition a few weeks ago at which he benched an incredible 620 weighing 232.

These days, when Mike is specializing in the bench, which is most of the time, he uses the following routine. He goes heavy each time he trains, using the same workout each training session. Recently, he made a training bench of 625 pounds, and the figures you see below are based on a top bench of 625.

Monday

Bench Press

$\left.\begin{array}{l} 135 \times 5 \\ 135 \times 5 \end{array}\right\}$ to get the feel of the bar

$\left.\begin{array}{l} 325 \times 1 \\ 325 \times 1 \\ 325 \times 1 \\ 425 \times 1 \\ 525 \times 1 \\ 625 \times 1 \end{array}\right\}$ concentrating on technique and form

On all of the above competition-style bench presses, Mike uses a 32-inch grip, which is the widest the rules allow. Following his heavy work, he moves his grip in to shoulder width and does two sets of three reps in movements which could be called sticking-point lockouts. He lowers the weight halfway down to approximately where the triceps take over from the chest and shoulders, and then drives it back overhead. It would be written as follows:

Sticking Point Lockout
475 × 3   475 × 3

Next, Mike uses the specially bent bar you see in one of the accompanying photos. He tells me that he used to do push-ups between chairs with extra weight on his shoulders until he became too strong for the movement to be practical, at which time he had the bent bar made to serve the same purpose. His reason for doing this exercise is that he believes it is far easier to develop a truly heavy bench press if you can find a shortcut to what he calls "blast-off power." He feels that the best way to encourage the chest muscles to build this sort of power is to stretch them more than they are stretched by a regular bench press. As you can see from the photo, the bar allows his hands to drop well below the level of the chest, thus placing a tremendous stretch on the pectoral muscles. He says that a 300-pound bencher should be able to handle around 225 on the special bar. When Mike does this exercise, he pauses for five seconds on the chest before each press. He says that when he finishes his chest is really burning from the work and the stretching. He uses the following weights:

Bent Bar Benches

435 × 3

435 × 3   using a five-second
pause on each rep.

435 × 3

That's it. No high repetition "pump set," no triceps presses, no arm work of any sort—only the tremendously heavy benches, the lockouts, and those chest stretchers, all done three times a week. Mike has of course experimented with all sorts of routines and exercises over the years, but he figures that the routine he's on now is the best he's ever used. There is one crucial point that I now need to make because Mike considers it extremely important. The point is that although Mike *usually* trains three times each week (Monday, Wednesday, and Saturday) on the bench, sometimes he will vary this, *depending on how well he feels the muscles of the arms, shoulders, and chest*

AT WORK IN his store in Duluth, Minnesota, Mike snacks throughout the day to keep his power and his energy level on a high plane.

have recovered. If he feels they are completely recovered, he trains; if he feels they need another day's rest, they get another day's rest.

He has a method of determining whether or not the muscles have recovered, and he recommends this method to everyone. He simply takes a broomstick on the morning of his scheduled workout, holds it out in front of his chest, then brings it slowly toward the chest, until it is touching. If he feels any soreness in the pectoral or front deltoids (shoulder muscles), he will do no benches that day because he believes that the soreness indicates that the muscles aren't fully recovered and that if you work a muscle group which isn't fully recuperated, you not only fail to make as much progress as you might but you also greatly increase your tendency to injure yourself.

In the past, Mike has made good use of the triceps press that you see pictured in this chapter. His method of performance is to lower the bar behind, and a few inches below, the top of his head and then triceps press it to arms' length. When he uses this exercise he handles the following poundages:

Triceps Press

135 × 10	305 × 6
205 × 6	255 × 6
255 × 6	

Another exercise he claims has been very beneficial to him is done by lowering the bar to a position one or two inches below the sticking point (the point of poorest leverage), then holding it there for about five seconds before forcing it through the sticking point and on up to arms' length.

Amazingly, *he never works his lats or his biceps,* two of the areas most big benchers really hit hard. Most top men train the lats and the biceps on what seems to me the sound theory that thicker arms at the elbow and more lattisimus

mass under the triceps provide better leverage, sort of a launching pad from which the bar is driven overhead. Even without this work, however, Mike's launching pad seems to be in fairly good order.

ONE OF MIKE'S assistance exercises is the standing triceps press.

Since most of you who are reading this book will not want to concentrate only on the bench but will want to increase your other lifts as well, I've asked Mike to provide you with the schedule he uses when he's training all three lifts. The schedule goes as follows:

Monday
Bench Press Workout
(as already given)

Tuesday
Squat

135 × 5	475 × 3
225 × 5	545 × 3
315 × 3	615 × 3
405 × 3	525 × 5

Wednesday
Bench Press Program
same as Monday, if muscles have recovered

Saturday
Bench Press Program
same as Monday and Wednesday
Squat
same as Tuesday
Deadlift

135 × 5	545 × 1
315 × 1	615 × 1
405 × 1	655 × 1
475 × 1	525 × 5

When Mike is on this program (as he is as this is being written), you can see that he trains as hard as before on the bench press: he simply lowers his expectations a bit since he is sensible enough to realize that his supply of energy is not unlimited and that some of the work and energy he lavished on the upper body when he was specializing will be soaked up by the large muscles of the thighs, hips, and lower back as he trains his squat and deadlift. He hopes to hold his bench press above 600 at a bodyweight of 220.5 for the 1977 National Championships, which he feels he has a good chance to win.

Even though Mike has decided to work hard on all the lifts for a while, however, those of us who know him well expect him to return after the Nationals to a program of specialization in the bench press. He really loves the lift, and his goals are to continue training and breaking records for at least another ten years. He expects to bench 650 as a 242-pounder before too long, and then he feels he'd like to creep up to the mind-numbing figure of 700 pounds as a light super-heavyweight, weighing 250 to 265. When I asked Mike about retirement, he said, "you will find that I am not a lifter who comes and goes quickly like most of them do. I am only 28 years old, and I

plan on setting new world records for many, many years."

When we last talked, he stressed the point again and again that beginners and intermediates should always remember that a person doesn't have to be naturally huge to hold records in powerlifting. As an example of this, he says that had he never trained with weights, he'd weigh around 165 pounds at a height of 5-feet 5-inches, and with his tiny (6.75 inch) wrists, he seems to be walking proof of his own argument. In Mike's view, the most important thing for a beginner to do is to train the lifts with *absolute strictness* and to be extremely careful not to sustain an injury. It's that week after week, month after month steady training, uninterrupted by injuries, that makes for championship lifting. In ten years of powerlifting, Mike has only been hurt once, a leg injury in last year's National Championships.

As far as grip width is concerned, Mike favors a 32-inch grip, because he feels that the wider hand spacing allows the

MIKE CONSIDERS THIS specially made bar to be one of the things most responsible for his power in the bench press. It allows his hands to go below the level of his chest.

huge and powerful pectoral muscles of the chest to function most efficiently. He realizes, however, that this is an individual matter that each lifter will have to determine for himself. In general, however, he feels that beginners should use as wide a grip as is comfortable for them, for he believes it will pay off in the long run.

Mike keeps his feet close together when he benches and when his bodyweight is in the 180-200-pound range he is able to arch his back a bit for better leverage. In the 220- and 242-pound classes, however, his thicker body doesn't seem to want to arch and so he lies almost flat on the bench. This doesn't worry him. As he told me, "The power I gain from the extra bodyweight more than makes up for the loss of leverage." He attempts to keep his upper arms at an angle of approximately

CHALKING HIS HANDS and psyching himself for the effort, Mike prepares to set another record in the bench press.

45 degrees to his upper body as he lowers the weight, allowing them to swing quickly out to almost 90 degrees when the bar gets halfway up. As he lowers the weight, he is very careful to touch the bar down on exactly the right spot for him, which is high on the chest, allowing the big pectorals to provide maximum "blast-off power."

Mike has other places to get his "blast-off power" besides his pectorals, as he is similar to most other top powerlifters in his belief that diet is a large part of successful lifting. And being the owner and operator of a natural foods store, he's in an ideal position to get what he feels his body needs. Each day he takes a super-strength multiple vitamin tablet, 1,000 mg. of vitamin C, 30 dessicated liver tablets, and 400 international units of vitamin E. Also, he drinks a lot of fruit juice, nutriment, and liquid protein, and he eats meat, lots of tuna fish, nuts, fruits, and some raw vegetables. Being in the store all day, he snacks constantly, so much so that he told me with a laugh that he ate up most of his profits. When he wants to gain or lose weight, he either adds or cuts down on his carbohydrates.

How much Mike will eventually bench press is difficult to say, but set up the way he is now with a thriving though not physically demanding job, I see no reason why he won't make good on his promise to continue breaking records for the next 10 or 15 years. I've seen him hoist those big, big weights on those slender arms enough times now that he's made a believer out of me. Doug Young and Larry Pacifico, both of whom are among the top five benchers in the world, are awed by Mike's prowess, and those of us who have seen him lift have come to respect what he says and to respect his predictions. He is, after all, the greatest pound-for-pound bench presser in the history of powerlifting.

BOB PEOPLES, THE powerlifting pioneer from East Tennessee, was the first man to officially pull 700 pounds in the deadlift. The weight at the end of Bob's long arms is 719 pounds.

chapter 4
THE DEADLIFT

The deadlift is the great separator. Coming as it does at the end of a powerlifting meet, it carries with it the natural drama of being the lift that decides who wins and who loses. Because of this and because of the stark, primitive nature of the lift, it is by far the most popular lift with spectators. With a title on the line and first place riding in the balance, there's nothing in all sports quite like watching some old boy haul up one of those low-gear, eye-popping, jaw-tooth rattlers that seems to take 30 seconds to complete.

Until the development of the plate-loading barbell early in this century, there were almost no barbells which lent themselves to limit deadlifts. The older bars were often of one "fixed" weight and were almost always unknurled as well as being so thick that it would have been impossible for most men to hold as much with their hands as they could have pulled with

their back, hips, and legs. But with the knurled, thinner bars that could be plate-loaded, some big deadlifts began to emerge, with the biggest ones by far being done by the almost superhumanly strong Herman Goerner. So powerful was the big German that I've always suspected that the astronomical poundages he supposedly pulled kept his contemporaries depressed to the point that they lost most of their interest in the lift.

In any case, after Goerner passed from the scene, it wasn't until after World War II that another pioneer appeared and began breaking ground for the seeds that would before long grow into the mature sport of powerlifting. The pioneer of whom I write was, and very much still is, 180-pound Bob Peoples, a farmer from the rolling hills of East Tennessee who became the first amateur of any body-weight to officially deadlift 700 pounds.

After Bob finally hung it up, the deadlift continued to grow in popularity until it began replacing the curl in both the "odd lifts" in the U.S. and the "strength set" in Great Britain in the early 1960s. One of the easiest lifts to judge, it has become the powerlift most closely identified with the sport, even to the extent that the figures adorning the tops of powerlifting trophies are of a man doing a deadlift. In my judgment, this popularity is well deserved, for not only can an average person understand and identify with the lift, but it also develops the type of strength in the hands, back, hips, and legs which make any sort of sport or manual labor easier. Below I have listed the official IPF rules for this big daddy of the powerlifts.

Deadlift
1. The bar must be laid horizontally in front of the lifter's feet, gripped with an optional grip with both hands, and uplifted with one continuous motion until the lifter is standing erect. At the completion of the lift, the knees must be locked and the shoulders thrust back. The referee's signal shall indicate the time when the bar is held motionless in the final position.

Causes for Disqualification for the Deadlift
1. Any stopping of the bar before it reaches the final position.
2. Failure to stand erect.
3. Failure to lock the knees.
4. Supporting the bar on the thighs.
5. Any raising of the bar or any deliberate attempt to do so shall count as an attempt.
6. Any shifting of the feet during the performance of the lift.
7. Any raising of the heels or toes.
8. Lowering the bar before the referee's signal to do so.
9. Allowing the bar to return to the platform without maintaining control with both hands.

AS THE GREAT George Crawford watches from the side referee's chair, 178.5-pound Vince Anello completes a world-record deadlift, which has stood since 1970, and then throws out his hands in the Anello sign of triumph.

VINCE ANELLO

To powerlifters everywhere, there is one man who is associated more strongly—if I may use such a word—with one of the three competitive lifts than is any other lifter with any other lift. The man is Vince Anello and the lift is the deadlift. Mention the name Anello among powerlifting enthusiasts, and you conjure images of enormous loads of iron being pulled, of gravity seeming to lose her grip, of world records being treated with contempt. For the past six or seven years, Vince the invincible has *ruled* the deadlift, holding the 198-pound class record since 1970, the 181-pound class record since 1972, and the 220-pound class record since 1973.

Watching Vince haul up the big ones is one of the true highs of powerlifting, one of the things the fans come to see. Those who have seen him lift know that when he comes out onto the stage he'll be so wired he'll be *smoking*, and they know from experience that something will definitely move. Usually, of course, it's the barbell, but sometimes it's the flesh of Vince's palm, which simply tears away under the enormous strain. Either the barbell or the flesh—the back will not be denied.

And what a back it is—awesome in its musculature and frighteningly efficient in its construction. The Anello back is a short one made shorter still by its ability to bend outward without making a completed lift impossible. Although it's rather hard to describe, Vince's back, when viewed from the side, has a rather pronounced outward (backward) bulge, which is only evident when he is deadlifting a heavy weight (see the accompanying photographs). This bulge is caused by a mid-back "hinge" in the vertebral column which bends outward as his shoulders are pulled downward by the weight. This hinging "shortens" the back, and as the back is the chief lever-arm of

the body in the deadlift, it therefore greatly increases the leverage Vince is able to apply. He did nothing to develop this hinge—it's his as a gift from God.

But although he was simply *blessed* with this anatomical oddity, he has worked as hard as anyone in this book to develop the muscles, tendons, and ligaments that allow him to take *advantage* of his anatomy. God supplied the advantage; Vince supplies the work. They make quite a team.

STANDING NORMALLY, VINCE'S arms, shoulders, and legs stamp him as a strongman. But his upper body is not short relative to his legs.

Even for a world-class athlete, Vince is an unusually thoughtful and disciplined person. He realizes that success in powerlifting is primarily influenced by three things other than natural talent. Those three things are nutrition, exercise programs, and mental conditioning; in order to better understand the thoroughness with which Vince approaches the sport, I have similarly divided my discussion of his lifting philosophy.

Although this chapter will be primarily devoted to Vince's methods and ideas related to deadlifting, it would be confusing to discuss his various deadlift routines without explaining how they fit into his overall exercise program. Therefore, what I have listed below are the exact sets, repetitions, and poundages of all the exercises Vince used in the last week in March of 1977, approximately six weeks before he was scheduled to lift in a contest in California. When we talked about his routine, Vince asked me to stress the fact that he felt that the amount of work he did for his back would be too much even for the average advanced powerlifter. He told me that several of his training partners had tried to follow his program of back work and had either gone stale, gotten injured, or both. As for Vince, evidently his unusual back structure allows him to handle more work. "I thrive on it," he told me. Here it is:

Monday

Squat

300 × 10	500 × 3
380 × 5	525 × 3
450 × 4	570 × 3

Bench Press

225 × 10	365 × 3
315 × 5	410 × 3
335 × 3	

Partial Bench Press
  (4-inch lockouts)

450 × 1	525 × 1
500 × 1	

Partial Deadlift
  (from just above the knee)

515 × 10	750 × 1
620 × 5	800 × 1
700 × 1	850 × 1

(all done without straps)

Tuesday

Press Behind Neck

135 × 6	230 × 6
175 × 6	230 × 6
205 × 6	

Lying Triceps Press

135 × 6	225 × 6
175 × 6	225 × 6
205 × 6	

Curl
  (done without much rest between sets)

115 × 6	115 × 6
115 × 6	115 × 6
115 × 6	

Triceps Press-Down on Lat Machine

100 × 6	150 × 6
130 × 6	150 × 6
140 × 6	

Lat-Machine Pulldown

150 × 6	300 × 6
200 × 6	300 × 6
250 × 6	

(amazing, no?)

Bent Forward Row

225 × 6	350 × 6
275 × 6	350 × 6
325 × 6	

Wide-Grip Chin Behind Neck
3 sets of 20 chins

Wednesday

Bench Press

225 × 10	400 × 1
315 × 5	430 × 1
365 × 1	440 × 1

Deadlift
  (without straps)

400 × 10	730 × 1
550 × 5	800 × 1
650 × 1	

Bent-Legged Good Morning

200 × 6	400 × 6
275 × 6	400 × 6
350 × 6	

Continuous Tension Squat
  **(never straightening the legs
  all the way between repetitions)**

225 × 10	350 × 10
275 × 10	350 × 10
325 × 10	

Shoulder Shrug
(without straps)

350 × 6	500 × 6
425 × 6	500 × 6
500 × 6	

Friday
Close-Grip Bench Press

225 × 10	350 × 3
315 × 5	350 × 3

THESE SEQUENCE PHOTOS show Vince's starting, midpoint, and finishing positions. Note that at the midpoint he keeps the bar so close to his knees that the skin on his kneecap is pulled upward. Note also that in the final photo his back seems to shorten under the strain of the weight.

Close-Grip Bench-Press Lockouts
(4 inches)

365 × 3	430 × 3
400 × 3	

Saturday
Squat

300 × 10	575 × 1
380 × 5	605 × 1
450 × 3	635 × 1
525 × 2	

Half Squat

650 × 1	820 × 1
750 × 1	

Quarter Squat

900 × 1	1200 × 1
1050 × 1	

Partial Deadlift—without straps
(about 3–4 inches higher
than normal height of bar)

400 × 10	750 × 1
515 × 5	820 × 1
660 × 1	

Bent-Legged Good Morning
same as Wednesday
Continuous Tension Squat
same as Wednesday
Bent Forward Row
same as Tuesday
Shoulder Shrug
same as Wednesday

Vince is no different from most other top lifters in his use of a cyclical approach to training, although he's a bit unusual in that he takes no layoffs throughout the year. He trains hard all 12 months, but he does vary his sets and reps, as follows. In the deadlift, if there are four or five months to go before a contest, Vince uses between five and seven sets, beginning with a set of ten with 50 percent of his best single. Next, he would add 70 pounds and do six reps, then 60 more for five reps, followed by 60 more for four reps, and 60 again for two or three sets of three.

EVEN THOUGH THE weight being lifted is "only" 500 pounds, these sequence photos show the "hinge" in Vince's back which gives him a slight leverage advantage.

Then, with the target contest three months away, Vince cuts his repetitions back to two on the final two or three sets, but he adds 90 pounds instead of 60. Two months before, he moves into a single repetition program, doing sets of ten, six, five, three, and three sets of one with limit or near-limit weights. Finally, one month to six weeks before the big meet, he's ready for his special "peaking" routine, which is the one listed for him on his Wednesday workout: a set of ten with 50 percent, a set of six with about 150 pounds more, followed by three singles with increasingly heavy weight so that the last single is at or very close to his limit. To give you an example of the absolutely gargantuan back strength of this relatively small (5-feet 5.5-inches, 215-pound) man, let me list the poundages he worked with on his heaviest day before the 1976 World Championships. He started with his customary 400 × 10, then jumped to 550 × 6, moved on to 700 × 1 and 800 × 1 before finishing with the almost unbelievable weight of *880 pounds,* a weight no

other man except 6-feet 4-inches 360-pound Don Reinhoudt has ever pulled.

The only problem about the 880, as Vince is now quick to admit, was that it was done with wrist straps to assist the grip. Although he recalls that he pulled the 880 rather easily, he feels that the lift filled him with false confidence about how much he could pull *without* straps and it contributed to a softening of the skin and flesh of his palms, making them more susceptible to tearing. At the time he trained at a gym which had a bar with very little knurling and because of the smoothness of the bar he was *forced* to use straps because he simply couldn't otherwise hang onto his heavy deadlifts and pulling exercises.

And so as the muscles of his back thickened and grew stronger from his long hours of pulling the smooth, knurl-free bar, his hands grew soft—not *weak,* but *soft.* He guarded against weakness by working with his usual zeal and regularity on a gripper, doing hundreds of repetitions to strengthen his hands and forearms. He even sought to avoid the softening by soaking his hands in brine, but without the callousing effect of regular work with a heavily knurled bar, Vince's hands simply became unable to stand the strain at the World Championships. Actually, his right palm tore in the warm-up room, and even with the palm heavily taped he was barely able to succeed with his opening attempt. He needed 837 to tie Great Britain's Paul Jordan and win by virtue of lighter bodyweight, and had his *hands* been in shape there's very little doubt he could have pulled it off.

But they *weren't* in shape, and thus he lost a championship he otherwise would almost certainly have won. This costly lesson wasn't wasted on Vince, however, and with the resilience which is typical of him, he went back home, bought a new, deeply knurled bar, and began again to train. He threw his straps away. This new approach to hand conditioning seems to be working really well for him, and he's gone over 800 several times in both his deadlifts and his partial deadlifts, using only his now-toughened hands to hold the

weight. At this point in his progress in the deadlift, his hands are his limiting factor. He feels that if his grip could hold 900 pounds, his back could lift it.

One of the methods he uses to maintain and develop his legendary back strength is to include partial squats—half squats and quarter squats—in his exercise program. He says that he originally used these exercises to help his squat, but while he noticed no improvement in the squat he *did* find that when his strength in the partial squat moved up, his *deadlift* moved up as well. Correspondingly, he found that when he discontinued the partial squatting, his deadlift suffered rather than his squat.

Another Anello "secret" is his concentration on upper-back or lat work in his training. Take another look at his routine, and you'll notice the severity of his lat training: five sets of six in the lat-machine pulldowns with a top weight of 300 pounds, five sets of six in the bent forward row with a top weight of 350 pounds, and for a final bit of touching up, three sets of 20 in the wide-grip chin behind the neck. He and Marty Joyce, another world-class deadlifter, both believe that a powerful shoulder girdle is a great asset in pulling the big ones and, for what it's worth, I agree.

AS TODD LOOKS on, trainer Karl Faeth applies tape to Vince's torn palm backstage at the 1976 World Championships.

A BIG PART of Anello's supplemental training is done on the power rack.

Although Vince usually uses five sets of six in his assistance exercises, he almost never goes over three reps in either the deadlift or the two partial deadlift positions. He feels that whereas the squat and bench press benefit from midrange (4-6) repetition work, the deadlift is another story, a *short* story, if you will. By far the majority of his deadlift training is made up of double reps or single reps, mostly singles. He told me that a couple of years ago a meet promoter asked him to give an exhibition by taking the top deadlift of the coming contest and doing as many repetitions with it as possible. "Foolishly," says Vince, "I agreed." The top weight handled was 650 pounds; so Vince marched out and lifted it ten times without stopping.

He said that although his back felt mined out, he didn't injure himself; so the following Saturday he worked up to his usual heavy triple—this time with 800 pounds. More fatigue but still no trouble, until the next day when he stretched out on a cold metal bench while wearing only a light T shirt. He laughs about it now, saying that the spasm which gripped his lumbar muscles was so extreme that he couldn't get his breath and thought he

was having a heart attack. He's never pushed reps again and he recommends that beginners also avoid high reps in the deadlift, staying between three and five. He suggests that a good beginner's routine would be to start with 50 percent of limit for ten reps, then go to 60 percent for eight, and on to 70 percent for three sets of five, training the lift twice each week and testing for limit every couple of months.

Obviously, Vince is a hard worker, a powerlifter who has evolved a complex, highly individualized program of exercise which is essential to his consistent success. But as hard as he works, and as important as his routine is to his success, *he considers diet to be three times more important.* Of all the lifters who are featured in this book, no one is as careful about diet as Vince, not even Mike Mac-Donald, who *owns* a natural foods store. Vince argues that if you plan to shock the body with regular bouts of heavy exercise, you must feed it with great thoughtfulness.

In the past, particularly when he would drop back into the 181-pound class, Vince has had trouble with his exercise-diet relationship. He said that as a lightheavy-

POSSESSOR OF SOME of the widest and strongest latissimus dorsi muscles in the world, Vince can use over 300 pounds in the pulldown.

ANOTHER ANELLO FAVORITE for working the upper back is these specialized rowing motions.

weight (181) he was forced to fast for three days each week in order to stay near the limit and that this self-denial made it impossible for the tearing down of the muscles through exercise to be balanced out by the intake of protein-rich food. He was also unhappy with various extreme, low-carbohydrate diets that he used from time to time, because they seemed to provide him with insufficient energy for his body-shocking workouts.

Finally, through trial and error, he has evolved a diet that provides him with adequate protein to build muscle and adequate carbohydrates to supply energy. He doesn't like to carry much fat; so he takes in just enough carbohydrates to fuel his big engine, not enough to have any left to be stored. Basically an average Anello daily diet would be about like this:

Breakfast:
one pound of meat, usually beef
two eggs
one banana
two oranges or a grapefruit

Mid-Morning Snack:
one can of tuna fish
one apple
a wedge of cheese

Lunch:
one and one-half pounds of meat, chicken, or fish
vegetable salad
one pint of milk
fresh fruit of some sort

Mid-Afternoon Snack: (4:00 P.M.)
Dried fruit and nuts with honey poured over it

Dinner (10:00 P.M.)
two pounds of meat, usually beef
vegetable salad

As Vince himself says, he eats to lift. He believes that one or two big meals a day are less efficient than six smaller ones, because the small meals are more easily assimilated by the digestive system. "It's not how much you *eat* that's important, it's how much you *assimilate*," he argues. In order to be certain that he assimilates the large amount of food he eats every day, he uses various digestion aids, such as hydrochloric acid (to aid in the digestion of protein) and Trienzyme (to aid in the digestion of proteins, fats, and starches) after every meal.

He's also a big fan of dessicated liver tablets, starting with 40 a day a month and a half before a big meet and building up to 200 a day by the time of the contest. Not only does he feel an energy boost from these tablets, but they also seem to help him increase his bodyweight. And to be sure he gets the maximum benefit from his liver tablets he always takes a little hydrochloric acid at the same time as he takes his liver. He also takes Progest because he feels it helps the body to maintain a positive nitrogen balance in much the same way as steroids.

Vitamins and minerals also play their part in Vince's master plan; for example,

VINCE USES THE bent-legged good morning exercise to improve his deadlift. Note that he uses his deadlifting shoes so that his legs are worked in the most appropriate way.

vitamins C and E, used daily, with the dosage often being as high as 5,000 units each. He also takes RNA and DNA, along with chelated minerals, zinc sulfate (for soreness), amino acids, calcium, and a general purpose B Complex. It goes without saying that the amount and variety of food and supplements that Vince takes is quite costly, but he reasons that as he neither drinks nor smokes and has very few doctor bills it all evens out.

One of the reasons he decided to move up into the 220-pound class is that he felt the heavier bodyweight would allow him to "feed" his body as he thinks he should for maximum gains. Even though he wants to gain, he avoids white sugar and white-flour products, and in the winter he avoids milk because it tends to increase the buildup of mucus in his throat. He also keeps his intake of eggs rather low so as to prevent any possibility of a cholesterol problem. In short, his diet is thorough, thoughtful, tailor-made and, when looked at in one way, rather expensive. When looked at in another way, however, it seems like a bargain. After all, in powerlifting, as in life, there's no such thing as a free lunch.

Besides Vince's elaborate nutrition program and his heavy-duty exercise routine, there is *another* aspect of his approach to powerlifting which he feels is absolutely essential to his success. He calls it "programming the mind." To begin with, it involves maintaining what Bob Hoffman always called a "tranquil mind." In order to reach a high level of mental tranquility, Vince practices Transcendental Meditation. Twice a day he meditates, and he says it has made a great difference in how relaxed he feels, particularly in the afternoon after a long day teaching school.

Following his meditation, he "programs" himself for his future workouts and contests in the following way. First, he lies on a flat surface, then tenses and relaxes each muscle group individually. As he tenses the various muscle groups, he *visualizes* them, attempting to inhabit them with his mind. When all the groups have been tensed and relaxed, he begins a countdown from 25 and when he reaches the count of "one" he visualizes himself ascending into the clouds, as if he were riding a giant escalator. Next, he imagines himself floating softly on the clouds for a few leisurely moments before riding slowly back to earth, counting from ten to one as he descends.

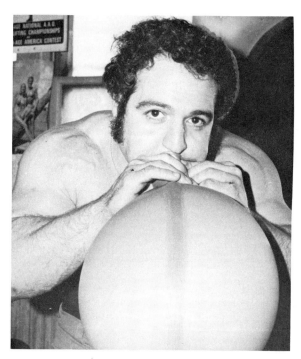

FROM TIME TO time Vince has given lifting exhibitions in which he concludes his show by blowing up a hot water bottle until it breaks.

At this point he's *really* relaxed and ready to be programmed. His initial step is to visualize the first exercise he plans to do in his next workout. He pictures the weight, the room, and himself taking the weight, fighting it, and succeeding with it for the planned number of repetitions. Using this technique, he goes completely through the program of exercise he has scheduled for his following workout. When he has imagined himself getting the last rep of the last set of the last exercise, he gets up, full of confidence that his visualizations will soon come to pass.

This autosuggestion he uses is, of course, a form of hypnosis. He feels it is a key to his progress because it gives him the confidence and incentive he needs to handle the world-record poundages he tackles during almost every workout. He has read widely in the field of hypnosis and although he warns that it is a serious business and not a thing for casual experimentation, he has also used various hypnotic techniques on his training partners, with good success. He regularly hypnotizes his buddy Jack Sidaris, who is also a nationally ranked 220-pounder. Once he puts Jack "under," he "programs" his partner's mind by suggesting to him the lifts he should make at whatever meet is forthcoming.

Vince believes that the positive frame of mind he maintains with his Transcendental Meditation and autosuggestion is *especially* important in the deadlift, the "psyche lift," he calls it. To illustrate the crucial function of the mind in the deadlift, he told me that he once successfully opened his deadlifts at 750 pounds in a contest after failing to pull 600 the week before in practice. Of course this was unusual for Vince because he generally performs well in both workouts and meets, as indicated by the following partial list of his "best" in training and in competition.

	181-pound class	198-pound class	220-pound class
Squat:	540 (official)	600 (official)	660 (official)
			650 (training)
Bench Press:	380 (official)	415 (official)	460 (official)
			450 (training)
Deadlift:	751 *(official)	804 *(official)	811 *(official)
			835 (training)

*Official world record.

Among Vince's future goals as a 220-pounder are a 700 squat, a 500 bench press and a 900 deadlift for the world-record total of 2,100 pounds. These goals are important to him, as he uses them to energize himself for his training. Even his daily workout goals are used in the same way: they give him a target which, if reached, makes the *next* target easier. Through the years Vince has used these methods to bring his deadlift up from the 400 pounds he made at his first competition. He was 19 years old at the time and was competing in bodybuilding, and for quite awhile he lifted simply because the bodybuilding contests were held in conjunction with the ones in powerlifting.

Nevertheless, he made good progress, going from the 400 to 470 at his second contest and then on up in successive meets to 470, 500, 510, 560, 600, 630, and 640, where he finally got stuck. These weights were all made as a 181-pounder, and he made them all using the narrow-grip, wide-stance sumo style. One day a friend who was watching him train urged him to try the more customary style, and Vince liked it so well he worked up to 670 that afternoon. Then, he moved up into the 198-pound class, lifting became his primary interest, and he began to rewrite the record books. For him 1970 was a good year.

In April of 1970, he deadlifted 705, then increased this record by hoisting 717 at the National Collegiates in May, only to move it up again to 724 as he won the Junior Nationals and to 740 in December. In early 1971, he made 775, adding five pounds eight months later. In 1972, he went back down to 181 and made 730 in the Senior Nationals, increasing that record to 735 two months later in winning the 1972 World Championships. A year later he made his last contribution to the 181-pound record books when he made his 751.

Though 1974 was a bad year for Vince, he came back hungry in 1975 and made his historic and never to be forgotten 804 record at the Senior Nationals in the 198-pound class. Then in 1976 he made a wise move and edged up into the 220-pound class where he was able to catch Marvin Phillips with a show-stopping 800-pound second attempt and win the Nationals. He made an 805 world record in Canada in January of 1977, and then moved that up to 811 in the spring, adding a 660 squat and a 460 bench for a best ever total of 1,930. Vince is most definitely not on the way out.

One reason why I say that is because he's a big fan of England's Ron Collins, whose astronomical lifting at the supposedly advanced age of 43 has caused powerlifters everywhere to revise their retirement timetables. Another reason Vince will probably be around for awhile is that he *enjoys* powerlifting so much. In the words of W. B. Yeats, he is compelled by "the fascination of what's difficult." When I asked him to describe the highlights of his lifting life, he smiled and went through all his major championships and world records and then added, "and of course all my training records—I've enjoyed them just as much."

He told me also that he really cherished the friendships he has made through powerlifting and that he feels he has grown and matured as a person as a result of his years of involvement with the sport. "I've learned how to handle disappointment," he said. "I've learned lessons by winning, but I've learned even more through defeat: how to train for months and years for a contest only to be beaten and to have to start all over and build again from scratch. My years of making weight and my regularity now in eating and training habits have helped make me a more disciplined person. When I was in college I remember many nights when

FROM OUT OF the past comes this picture of teenaged Vince Anello taken when he was concentrating on bodybuilding. Even then his back looked like it was built for big weights.

others stayed out late and I was in bed early so that I'd be ready for my next workout. These habits have carried over into other areas of my life, and perhaps I'm more able to make good use of my limited time. I love the beach and I love the ladies and I love to ride my motorcycle, but I love lifting more—and I'm willing to sacrifice for it."

Through his reputation as a powerlifter, Vince has had a powerful influence on the lives of many young people, and he's proud of this influence. He told me about one classic case in which a woman had called him about her son, who was so small (5-feet 4-inches and 95 pounds) that he was picked on. The woman had read that Vince himself was not very tall (5-feet 5.5-inches), but that he had a 54-inch chest, 29-inch thighs, and a neck and arms which measured 19.5 inches, so she asked for Vince's help and he wrote the boy a dietary and exercise program which has been followed so diligently through the last several years that his weight went from 95 to 180. He's a competitive powerlifter now himself, and he and Vince still correspond. Naturally, Vince treasures such experiences.

The fact that he has often been an inspiration to young lifters and the fact that for years he has been a big name in powerlifting hasn't meant that he has lost the capacity to admire other people.

VINCE GIVES A lift to a couple of young women who are training under his direction on the powerlifts.

When I asked him about this he named several men whose careers had inspired him, but the one person he singled out over all others was Larry Pacifico. "To me," Vince said, "Larry typifies the ideal powerlifter. Not only is he a great lifter, but he's also a success in his profession and a widely respected man, a real gentleman." As Vince said these things about Larry I had to hide my smile, not because I disagree, but because this description of Pacifico could just as easily fit *another* widely respected man, a man who is history's greatest deadlifter, pound for pound, Vincent Anello.

DON REINHOUDT

Much has been written through the years, some of it by me, about just exactly who is, or was, the strongest man in the world. As of 1977, many people feel that the title still belongs in the meaty paws of 44-year-old Paul Anderson, the famed Dixie Derrick, but most Olympic lifters would argue that their own great champion, Vasily Alexeev, deserves it more. And competitive powerlifters, of course, contend that they have a man who is stronger than either Anderson *or* Alexeev, stronger than anyone who has ever lived. That man is the 6-feet 3.5-inch, 360-pound Don Reinhoudt, Superheavyweight Powerlifting Champion of the World since 1973, holder of the world record in the squat (with 935), the deadlift (with 885), and the total (with 2,420).

Although this is neither the time nor the place to examine the question of who, *if anyone*, can be truly said to be the world's strongest man, it still seems fair to point out that in the deadlift, the most basic and simple test of overall bodily strength in existence, no one has ever done as much as big Don. I was there the day he pulled the 885, and let me tell you I was impressed. At my best, I could

ONE OF THE most dramatic moments in powerlifting history occurred in November 1976 when big Don Reinhoudt took 904 pounds for his farewell lift as a superheavyweight. With good friend Larry Pacifico at the microphone urging on the crowd, Don came out and, as the photos clearly show, almost completed the monstrous weight.

deadlift 800 pounds and once, using straps, I pulled 900 pounds a couple of inches off the floor; so I knew more than most what an awesome weight it was that Don had hauled all the way up to the top. The day I almost busted a gusset to break that 900 loose I remarked to one of my training partners that although I guessed that someone, someday, would pull 900 all the way up, it sure as hell wasn't going to be me.

I was also there the afternoon down in Texas at the 1976 Nationals when Don pulled 860 so easily that I'd lay money that on that day he could've made the big nine. He told me the day after he'd won his fourth consecutive world title that the feat of strength of which he was most proud was that 860 deadlift. Even though his 885 was heavier, he felt better about the 860 because it was made at a National meet and because he had pulled it so

strongly. We had a long talk—one of many we've had over the years—the day after the 1976 World's, and naturally our talk centered on the deadlift, not only because of Don's historic swansong attempt at 900 less than 24 hours before but because, to us, the lift in itself is so fascinating.

The evening before I had been deeply disappointed by Don's failure to complete the 900, but I knew that my disappointment was nothing compared to what he was feeling after having trained so long and so hard with the idea in mind to go out in high style—to let his last official lift as a competitive superheavyweight be a three white-light deadlift with the barrier weight of 900 pounds. "Give them something to remember the big guy," he was thinking. And he damn near pulled it. For my part, I would've given $100 to have seen him make it because if there was ever a kindlier, more gracious, or gentler giant than Don or a more jovial ambassador for our sport I've never met him. He *deserved* to make it.

AN EARLY PICTURE of Don taken after about a year of training. He weighed 235 then, and his best deadlift was 505.

I'm no different from most folks in that I like storybook endings and had Don pulled that 900 on the last attempt of the last lift in the last contest of his long career, with the whole crowd up stomping and shouting for him as his old friend Larry Pacifico urged them on over the microphone by announcing that the attempt at 900 would be his farewell lift, it would have been the kind of ending in keeping with Ernest Hemingway's advice that a champion should go out on a particularly good day.

As Don and I reviewed the training he had done for the meet, I felt even sorrier for the big man because if there ever was a batch of "best laid plans," it was his program of cyclical increases leading up

to the assault on the 900. Normally, his program calls for bench presses twice a week (Tuesday and Friday), squats twice a week (Wednesday and Saturday) and deadlifts once a week (Wednesday). During the last five weeks of heavy training before the meet, however, he dropped his Saturday squatting so that he could really load on the iron on Wednesday and give his legs, hips, and back a full week to recover.

During those final five weeks, he used the following weights, sets and repetitions:

First Week

Squat

245 × 5	760 × 2
445 × 2	805 × 3
645 × 2	865 × 1

Deadlift

245 × 5	760 × 2
445 × 2	805 × 3
645 × 2	

Second Week

Squat

245 × 5	760 × 2
445 × 2	810 × 3
645 × 2	875 × 1

Deadlift

245 × 5	760 × 2
445 × 2	810 × 3
645 × 2	

Third Week

Squat

245 × 5	760 × 2
445 × 2	815 × 3
645 × 2	885 × 1

Deadlift

245 × 5	760 × 2
445 × 2	820 × 1
645 × 2	

Fourth Week

Squat

245 × 5	760 × 2
445 × 2	820 × 3
645 × 2	900 × 1

Deadlift

245 × 5	760 × 2
445 × 2	860 × 1
645 × 2	

Fifth Week

Squat

245 × 5	760 × 2
445 × 2	825 × 3
645 × 2	920 × 1

Deadlift

245 × 5	760 × 2
445 × 2	880 × 1
645 × 2	

That monumental fifth-week session in which he totalled 1,800 pounds without even bench pressing was done two and a half weeks before the scheduled contest. He tapered down to the meet in the following way:

Eleven days before

Squat

245 × 5	645 × 2
445 × 2	760 × 2

AT 6 FOOT 3.5 INCHES and 360 pounds, the biggest man in the history of competitive lifting cinches up his belt before taking a 900-pound squat.

Deadlift

245 × 5	645 × 2
445 × 2	760 × 1

Seven days before

Squat

245 × 5	645 × 2
445 × 2	760 × 1

Deadlift

245 × 5	645 × 1
445 × 2	

Besides the awesome weights he handles, several other things about Don's deadlift training are unusual, such as the fact that he always uses straps in training, gripping the bar with his hands only in the meets. What's more, he never in any way trains his grip, simply relying on his huge hand size and great strength to keep the bar from slipping. Actually, part of the reason he always uses the straps is *because* of the size and thickness, the *meatiness*, of his hands. His palms are so fleshy that he is understandably fearful that his hands would tear if he trained the deadlift without straps. Amazingly, his grip has never failed him.

Another unusual aspect of his training is his almost preposterous weight increases between sets. On his heaviest deadlift training day, he made successive jumps of 200 pounds, 200 pounds, 115 pounds, and 120 pounds—far more than usual, even for superheavyweights. His argument is that these huge jumps save his energy for the really heavy final single. He says that if you wear proper workout clothes so that you stay warm, all you need to do is enough exercise to be sure that the muscles are sufficiently warm to handle a maximum attempt. He also feels that this technique gets his mind right for a big meet in that he doesn't need the usual large number of warm-up attempts. He says it keeps him hungry for the big ones.

And speaking of being hungry, now might be a good time to discuss the vict-

EVEN THOUGH THESE sequence shots were taken after he had lost 100 pounds of body weight, they still serve to illustrate his basic deadlift style, particularly his deep position at the beginning of the lift.

uals it takes to build 365 pounds worth of muscle and blood, although the average person will no doubt be surprised by the fact that Don is like most superheavyweights in that his average daily food intake was probably in the 5000-7000 calorie range. Nowhere in his diet will you find whole suckling pigs or roasted turkeys eaten at a single sitting and nowhere will you find gallon after gallon of milk. The era of the legendary trenchermen seems to have died with the likes of Louis Cyr, Horace Barre, and Louis Uni, men who thought nothing of going through ten pounds of meat in a day along with

all the trimmings. Uni was once reported to have remarked to a waiter in a Paris restaurant after having eaten a filet mignon, "The sample was exquisite. Now bring me the dinner."

All this is not to say that Don and other supers don't do a far better than average job of hiding the groceries, but those of you who want to add bodyweight should be pleased to learn that size can be gained without rupturing either your stomach *or* your pocketbook. As Don trained through the years he concentrated on what can only be called standard American food: he ate lots of meat of various kinds, lots of vegetables, and he drank his share of milk. In addition, he has used predigested protein for the last couple of years as he cut back on his milk in an effort to avoid the bloated feeling which so often accompanies the swilling of glassful after glassful of the wonderful white stuff.

At least part of the reason for Don's success in gaining weight was the *regularity* with which he ate, trained, and rested. Don is no different from most champions. He is *disciplined*. When his program called for him to train, he trained; when his diet called for him to eat, he ate; and when his schedule called for him to rest, he rested, sleeping eight to nine hours each night. If any single thing can be said to be the secret of making gains in size and strength, that one single thing is

regularity. Don did *not* miss workouts, and he rarely, if ever, failed to get his required amount of food and sleep. Without this enormous capacity for self-discipline, no amount of natural talent would have made him a champion.

And while I'm on the subject of the various things which helped big Don set 20 world records and dominate the super-heavies for the last four years, I want to be sure to give the proper amount of credit where credit is due, because he didn't do it alone. He couldn't have done it without his coach. He couldn't have done it without his longtime training partner, and he couldn't have done it without his masseuse. Fortunately for Don and fortunately for lifting, his wife not only isn't jealous of these close relationships, she *couldn't* be jealous of them

THESE PHOTOS SHOW the now trim Reinhoudt preparing to pull and then pulling the bar from several different pin settings or heights.

because they were with *her*. You see, Don's wife coaches him, lifts with him, and when she has a couple of hours to kill, rubs him down. (Rubbing him down would be rather like painting the Titanic, I'd imagine.)

For years, Don and Cindy have trained together, coaching one another in their basement gym as well as on the platforms of the world in international competition. In my time I've seen many close personal relationships in lifting, but I've never seen one as close as theirs. They are in fact such a marvelous team—both so big and strong and gentle—that when my wife and I bought a pair of draft horses we named them after the Reinhoudts. Of course, our Don weighs 2,000 rather than 360 and our Cindy 1,850 instead of 165, but when it comes to teamwork I'm afraid the four-legged namesakes are a distant second to their two-legged godparents.

People who have never seen Don perform are amazed to see this absolutely gargantuan man accompanied onto the stage by a handsome woman who hands him his chalk, adjusts his uniform, and then shouts encouragement to him as he prepares to lift. And the things she shouts are hardly the traditional wifely urgings of "C'mon, honey" or "You can do it" or whatever. Instead she yells such things as you'd *expect* a workout partner and coach to yell: "Stay tight!" "Blow it up now!" And so on. Personally, I find their relationship deeply touching.

Besides being such a smooth-working team, they are both really first-rate people, so open and generous with their time. Because of this, Don is immensely popular with the fans, a true people's champion. Sometimes, he seems almost *too* friendly, and his energy and concentration before a big meet are drained away by endless questions and requests for photographs from the hordes of fans who follow him wherever he goes. I remarked

once that he reminded me a bit of one of the large breeds of dog (St. Bernard, Newfoundland, Great Pyrenees, etc.) whose friendliness seems to spring from the realization that only in that way will they get their fair share of petting— basically, they are fearful that their size will frighten people. They seem to keep on wagging their tails and hoping that the effect of their size will be secondary to the effect of their friendliness. In Don's case, his friendliness is so open and transparently honest that his size *does* seem to diminish—to become somehow less threatening.

But don't doubt for a moment that he is a *spectacularly* big man. All-around, he is the biggest world-class lifter in Olympic *or* powerlifting history. Other men have perhaps been in some ways thicker, Anderson (5-feet 9.5-inches, 375 pounds), Reding (5-feet 8-inches, 320 pounds), Williams (6-feet 1-inch, 345 pounds); and others have been a bit taller, Pickett (6-feet 4.5-inches), Ambartsumian (6-feet 5-inches), but no other top superheavyweight has had the overall size of Donald Reinhoudt. Listen. He is between 6-feet 3-inches and 6-feet 4-inches tall and he has weighed as much as 380 pounds. Without exercising or "pumping up," his chest is 60 inches, his neck is 22 inches, and his upper arm is 22.75 inches. The most amazing measurement of all, however, is that of his monumental forearms. His wife measured his right forearm with his arm almost completely straight but with his wrist flexed to swell the forearm and the measurement she got was 18.5 inches. Lord have mercy! An 18.5-inch forearm!

The important thing is that I *believe* the measurement. I've seen all the big men of the past 20 years, and *none* of them have had forearms and wrists like Don. Of course none of them have had hands and feet like his either. Alexeev, for instance, wears a size 10 shoe, whereas

Don wears a 15 EEE. Anderson has enormously thick, broad hands but they aren't exceptionally long—Don's are thick, wide, *and* long. Even Don's *head* is unusually big, too big for even a size 8 hat. In short, his bigness is not all manufactured. He was *born* big and he just kept growing.

His father was also a big man, weighing 260 pounds at the time of his recent death; so Don came by his size honestly. In high school, for instance, before he'd ever touched a weight, he weighed 220 pounds in the middle of basketball season at the age of 17. So naturally when he began hitting the weights, the size came quickly as the muscles began to pack themselves into the nooks and crannies of his titanic frame. Don had weighed over 300 pounds for the past six or seven years, reaching the previously mentioned top bodyweight of 380 last year in training, but this past November after his retirement as a competitive superheavyweight, he decided to drop a hundred pounds or so.

ONE OF THE few men ever to reach 600 pounds in the bench press, Don rams 585.

When he got back home to Fredonia after winning the World's, he found that he weighed 365 pounds. That was November 10, 1976. On March 5, 1977, less than four months later, what was left of Don stepped on the scales and read that they registered 239 pounds, a loss of 125 pounds in less than 120 days. As you can see, when Don decides to do something

he *does* it, Jack. You can *depend* on it. At 239 he felt far too light; so he has let his weight slide back up to around 280, where he plans to remain in hopes that the proposed 275-pound class becomes a reality. He loves to compete, but he feels that he'd rather compete at the healthier weight of 275. The extra 100 pounds gave him great trouble as well as great strength. He was bothered by shortness of breath, lack of flexibility, and the continuing difficulty of being unable to do a lot of things that normal people do, such as bicycle riding, hiking, and fitting into regular seats in movies, restaurants, and airplanes. To be a superheavyweight is a sacrifice, and Don and Cindy both felt that four years at the top had been sacrifice enough.

As Don and I talked last November and again this past April when we were in New Hampshire to watch our wives lift, I tried to tell him what it has been like to be a retired superheavy—about the satisfactions and the sorrows of losing almost a third of yourself. As we talked, we came again to the topic that seems to us so endlessly absorbing, the deadlift. I asked Don to describe the man he felt would one day reach the seemingly unreachable weight of 1,000 pounds, and he said that he thought the *first* man to hoist a half ton would be a truly big man: tall and heavy, with large, powerful hands, a relatively short back, and an efficient deadlift technique. He said he knew of no one who was currently lifting who had the physical potential to make such a lift, but he agreed with me that among the ranks of pro football there must be a few men who could, with training, reach into four figures.

He told me about several of the Buffalo Bills who used to train with him and Cindy in Fredonia, one of whom was unable to deadlift 500 even though he was 6-feet 6-inches tall and weighed 285 pounds. We talked about Don's own amazing improvement in the deadlift—

from an awkward-looking lift in the low 600's to a majestic success with 885. I told Don that he had reversed the usual trend of the superheavyweights by making bigger gains in the deadlift through the years than in the squat. *Usually,* as big men gain they find that although the extra bodyweight provides far better leverage in the squat, it tends to hurt them in the deadlift by making it uncomfortable to bend over far enough and "sit" or squat low enough to have a solid starting position. This generally results in large increases in squat poundages and small increases (if any) in the deadlift. In 1972, for example, John Kuc gained 50 pounds in bodyweight from the year before (272 to 322) and although he put well over 100 pounds on his squat, he made no gains at all in the deadlift.

Don said he realized early in his career that this would be a problem for him; so he always worked extra hard on his bottom position, forcing himself to sit lower and lower until he was able to reach a point from which the great power of his legs and hips could be brought into play. He concentrated on keeping his heels close together but pointing his toes outward so that as he bent down to the bar his thighs would spread and allow his belly to pass between them, thus preventing the cramped feeling most supers have at the bottom of the deadlift. He also was careful to keep the bar as close to his shins and thighs as possible throughout the lift, therefore maximizing his leverage. Another trick he uses is to keep his head *down* during both the deadlift and the squat. In order to do this with full concentration, he simply focuses on the head referee's feet.

Other than the deadlift itself, Don has done no other assistance exercises besides partial deadlifts on the rack. He used these before the 1976 Nationals, pulling a best of 935 pounds from the knees up. He always did them on Wednesdays, following his regular deadlifts. And he usually

did six or seven sets of one repetition, starting at around 700 pounds and jumping 50 or 60 pounds per set. He has never done rows or power cleans or high pulls or shoulder shrugs, but he did experiment a bit with the good morning exercise some years ago. As in his squat and bench-press training, the big man likes his workouts *basic*—heavy and simple. Mainly heavy. His advice for beginners echoes this philosophy. He says that they should do the squat and bench press at least twice a week and the deadlift at least once and that they should concentrate on good technique, using midrange repetitions.

As we talked about various pretenders to his throne, Don had only praise for them, particularly for Doyle Kanady and Paul Wrenn. He realizes that his records, high as they are, will fall before the broom of history, and he thinks that Kanady and Wrenn have the best chance to do the sweeping. As this is being written, in fact, I've just heard that both Kanady and Wrenn have in the past couple of weeks attempted to exceed Don's squat record of 935 pounds. Though neither of them broke it, one of them soon will and this would leave only the total and the deadlift in the mighty mitts of the big man from New York. And before very long even those will pass, as mine have done, into the pages of record books and the memories of powerlifting fans. At that time, Don will be sustained by the same thing that sustains me, which is that for a longer time than most he was the best in the world. It will do.

DON HAS PROBABLY squatted with more than 900 pounds more often than anyone in history, and as this book is written he holds the record with 934.

THREE OF RON Collins' teammates from England: Eddie Pengelly, who recently broke the world squat and total records in the 132-pound class; Tony Fitton, Britain's 242-pound champ and Collins' training partner; and Paul Jordan, world 220-pound champion.

chapter 5
THE TOTAL

As exciting as it is either to see or to do a heavy squat, a record bench press, or a limit deadlift, the *important* thing in powerlifting is what that squat, that bench press, and that deadlift *total* when they're added together. It has been understood since the earliest days of competitive lifting that no one man could be stronger than all others in every possible lift and that the fairest way to determine strength was therefore to choose a group of lifts and then add up each lifter's best effort in each event so that the overall winner and strongest man would be the one who lifted the most *total* weight, regardless of whether he won the individual events.

Back in the salad days of lifting, the way things were often done in two-man contests was to let one man choose three or four or five of his favorite lifts and then let the other man choose an equal number of *his* favorites. In this way, if each man chose four lifts, the contest would be determined by the total weight lifted in eight lifts, as almost never would the contestants choose even one of the same lifts. Obviously, this approach was seriously flawed because neither man had much, if any, chance to practice on his opponent's lifts. Finally, the British Amateur Weightlifting Association, the French-based *Fédération International*

Haltérophile, and other amateur organizations began standardizing the major lifts so that people everywhere would have rules within which to train.

But even so, it was still the feeling of these various federations that *several* lifts should be chosen so that whoever won one of their contests could be said to have balanced, or all-around, strength.

One of the hardest things in powerlifting is to back off a bit on the training for your favorite (almost always this is also your *best*) lift in order to have the energy you need to bring up or maintain your other two lifts. Similarly, doing that extra two heavy sets of squats when you know it's going to drain you for your pet lift, the bench press, requires exceptional self-discipline and objectivity. *However*, these are the kinds of toughminded decisions without which maximum progress in the total—the all-important total—simply cannot be made. The great specialists of our sport are without question exciting to watch—at times even memorable—but the hearts of the real powerlifting fans belong to those athletes who harness their three lifts like a teamster would harness his draft horses, thus insuring that when any one of the three was asked to haul a big load, a big load would indeed be hauled.

RON COLLINS

To be honest, I'm getting more than a little bit sick of Ron Collins. Seems to me that a man with any decency at all would realize how he makes the rest of us retirees feel as he goes into his 43rd year stronger than ever and winning his fifth world championship with a new world-record total. Has he no sympathy for those of us who have to suffer through dozens of conversations such as the following?

"Hey there, aren't you Terry Todd?"

"That's me all right."

"Wow. I've read your articles. Are you here to cover the World Championships?"

"Yes, I'm here for that and to visit with some of my buddies."

"What about that Collins last night?"

"Too much. He's too much."

"I'll say. And to think he's 42 years old."

"Yeah, it's amazing, I'll admit."

"How old are you, Dr. Todd?"

"Almost as old as Jack Benny."

"Late thirties, huh?"

"Thereabouts."

"Do you still compete?"

"No, no. I haven't competed for ten years."

"Well, after seeing Collins lift, why not?"

"Look, you'll have to excuse me. Someone's calling me from the other side of the auditorium. Awfully nice talking to you."

After all, why can't he just lay back like the rest of us, do a little light training, get together with other old-timers at the big meets, lie about how much he lifted in contests past like we do, and just sort of take it easy? Not Collins. From the looks of things, he's going to keep on making it hot for us ex-heroes for quite awhile as he's planning to continue competing as long as he can continue making gains. I guess I and the other senior citizens will just have to learn to put up with him.

Being *really* honest, everyone in lifting, *especially* those of us who've racked it up, loves and respects Ron Collins, for in him we see, or like to see, what we all could be if we only had the will and the passion to live as Dylan Thomas urged when he said,

"Do not go gentle into that good night
But rage, rage against the dying of the light.

Which is how, just how, Ron Collins lives and how he lifts.

How did he begin, this man whom age does not wither? In a long talk we had in York following his most recent world title, he told me that at the age of 28, and a bodyweight of 145 pounds, he began to train with weights in order to increase his ability in soccer. Always naturally strong, he enjoyed training immensely; after a year he jilted soccer, for 20 years the love of his life, and fell heavily into the arms of the Iron Maiden, where he's been ever since.

By 1962, he was already strong enough to qualify for and win the British National "Strength Set" (Squat, Bench Press, and Curl) Championship, but he was busy with his job and didn't enter. But by 1966 the curl had been replaced by the deadlift, and Ron was ready not only to enter but to win his first National Championship. Since that time, 11 more National Championships have been held, and Ron has won every one of them, creating dozens of world records in the process.

As this is being written, he just finished polishing his image to an even higher sheen with his twelfth consecutive British title and his second world-record total in less than one month. On April 18, 1977, lifting in Finland, he did a 710.75 world-record squat, a 418.75 bench press, and a 688.75 deadlift for an 1,818.25 world-record total. Then, on June 15, in Birmingham, England, he increased his squat record to 716.5, benched the same 418.75, and upped his deadlift to 722 for an 1,857.25 total, which as I recall is higher than anyone but Larry Pacifico has ever made *in the class above*. Even so, those of us who know him realize that he'll be satisfied with nothing less than 1,900.

What routine could produce such regular, amazing, relatively injury-free progress? In our talk, he described his favorite routine, along with the maximum poundages he used before the 1976 World's.

Monday
Squat
One set of free squats

135 × 10	670 × 3
235 × 10	700 × 1
335 × 8	720 × 1
420 × 5	740 × 1
520 × 5	750 × 1
600 × 3	

Bench Press

135 × 8	405 × 3
225 × 8	440 × 1
330 × 5	375 × 5

Deadlift

330 × 5	620 × 3
440 × 5	650 × 1
520 × 3	680 × 1
600 × 3	690 × 1

(He has done 650 for five reps, but he usually stays with singles, doubles, and triples with a weight near his planned starting attempt.) It should be noted that although he used straps for a brief time, he does all his deadlifting now without them.

Wrist Curl
Light weight and high reps, rolling the weight down into the fingers.
Grip Machine
Light weight and high reps.

Wednesday
Dumbbell Press
Using 75-pound dumbbells, five sets of ten reps.
Bent Forward Rowing
Five sets of five with 25 pounds.

RON COLLINS, THE 43-year-old champion of champions, is shown here as he pulls close to 700 pounds in training.

Bench Press
Using a narrow (approximately 18 inch) grip, he works up in sets of five reps to 320 (his best is eight reps with the 320).

Curl
Four or five sets of five with light weights.

Friday

The same as Monday except that he works up to a limit with five reps in each of the three lifts rather than for triples or singles. His bests for five are: Squat, 680; Bench Press, 390; Deadlift, 650.

Wrist Curls
same as Monday

Grip Machine
same as Monday

He follows more or less this same routine for six weeks before the World Championships in early November, after which he takes a complete layoff from all exercise until January, when he will begin with light bodybuilding. From this, he gradually increases the poundages and narrows his focus so that finally the three powerlifts once again dominate his schedule. His weight has never exceeded 189, and he likes to keep his weight no higher than five pounds over the 181.75-pound limit. Weighing around 187-188, his best practice lifts in 1976 (750-440-690) gave

him a gym total of 1,880, and he was hoping to be near that at the World's. Figuring to lose quite a bit on the squat as he lost weight and to lose a little on the bench press, he was confident of having the strength to make 722-435-722.

In my opinion, and in the opinion of his good friend and coach, Tony Fitton, he *did* have the strength, as his 711 squat and 424 bench press were strongly done, even though they each drew two red lights. In the deadlift, of course, his 722 was done with power to spare. He feels, and I agree with him, that he is capable of a 1,900 total as a lightheavyweight. That is his immediate goal. After that, he is considering increasing his bodyweight and competing in the 198.25-pound class. As I said earlier, the boy ain't studying no retirement.

Besides my conversations and correspondence with Ron himself, I've exchanged quite a few letters with Tony Fitton, who probably understands and appreciates Collins' ability and training style better than anyone in the world.

COLLINS USES A bench press style in which the weight of his body and the bar rests primarily on his shoulders and feet. He does not "plant" his hips, but keeps them only lightly touching the bench throughout the lift. This provides maximum leverage, but it's a tricky style to use.

SURROUNDED, SPOTTED, AND supported by his training partners, Ron prepares to take a 700-plus squat in a practice session before his recent spree of record breaking.

These letters I've received from Tony are so filled with insight, wit, and a passionate love of powerlifting that I've decided to include several passages from them which help explain the nature and nurture of this phenomenal athlete.

"Going back to his Middleweight days, Ron never let his training bodyweight get more than five or six pounds over the limit; now as a 181-pounder the most he has weighed prior to a contest is eight pounds over the limit. He is not a great believer in making drastic weight reductions and then having the hassle and worry of trying to replace most of the lost fluid. He keeps his diet sensible yet substantial, and I believe that now, after two years at 181 he is just beginning to function properly at this weight. As you have witnessed, Ron has been troubled badly with cramps and this was by no means an isolated instance. He has had his worst cramp attack when he didn't need diuretics to make weight. Also during the two to three weeks prior to a contest, cramps occasionally occurred in training. Cramps have always been accredited to an electro-

lyte imbalance but such facts made our good friend and doctor—Tony Banks—think beyond the electrolyte factor. Tony is convinced that physiologically, powerlifters' muscles are different in certain ways from those of Olympic lifters. He therefore treated us with a drug called Praxilene Oxalate made by Lipha, U.K. The drug it actually contains is naftidrofuryl. The Praxilene Oxalate has seemingly totally eradicated *any* discomfort from cramps, let alone the debilitating effects experienced in the past. The dosage is 600 mg. daily two days prior to and on the day of the meet. Incidentally, I gave six tablets of Praxilene Oxalate to Doug Young last year when he was seemingly suffering from cramps very badly and he was completely recovered within three quarters of an hour. Unfortunately, I have been told that Praxilene Oxalate does not have a license in North America, for what reason I don't know.

"In any case, now that cramping problems have been sorted out, Ron is willing to take his bodyweight up to seven or eight pounds over the limit but no more

IN ORDER TO thicken and strengthen his shoulders, Ron often does side lateral raises on his "light" days. *(Right)* One of the "regulars" in his bodybuilding program is the bent forward row. Note that he does this 225 pounds without straps.

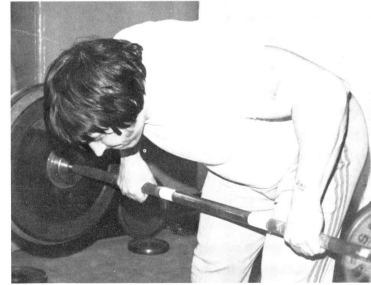

as he will not gorge or eat much after weigh-in and likes to have contests feel fairly similar in all respects to his training.

"Unlike other lifters, myself included, Ron has not taken too much interest in the medical aspect of lifting and lifting performances, and he certainly does not abuse anything that has been proved beneficial. Abuse is for lifters who don't believe in their own abilities. Ron definitely believes in his, and I feel right in saying that he resents the 'intrusion' of medical aides. Where he does concede he does so with moderation.

"After weigh-in he likes to relax, compose himself, and not worry about getting weight back on excessively or thinking his performance may be hampered by cramps, a bloated stomach, or a feeling of nausea or illness. To do this he keeps a constant check on his weight while eating good substantial food. If his bodyweight does start to drift a little too high during the weeks before a meet some of the luxuries of a lifter's diet—the occasional toast or piece of bread or sweet or pint of beer—have to be pruned off.

"In a lot of your accounts of Ron's lifting you remark about his clever use of the clock. With or without Ron's blessing I would like to give you some background on this point. Ron, either purposely or subconsciously, has set his pace of life on slow. He moves without any apparent haste, and he will not be rushed, flustered, or unnerved. He just plods along at his own selected speed—*slow*. He even drives his car carefully and unhurriedly. I can honestly say that at times I find him to be totally annoying in this respect. For instance, when we were browsing the shops in York's Mall before last year's Worlds we had to keep stopping so that Ron could catch up. He always seemed to be behind, lingering, not looking at anything in particular, just being *slow*.

"I'll never forget when I was the manager for one international trip with three-quarters of an hour to make Heathrow airport. The team was already assembled and the taxis had been waiting for a half hour and I had been worrying all the time about Ron. He was still not ready. Someone said that when he was last seen he was putting talcum powder on his arse. Finally he came down with his luggage, slowly, wondering what the panic was, saying, 'We'll make it alright, they won't go without us.' Well, they didn't go without us, but it probably took five years off my life.

"What's this got to do with clever use of the clock? Well, it's just that Ron will simply not lift till he feels ready and an inbuilt timing system seldom fails him. If I were to list some of Ron's special qualities, particularly ones which are apparent when he is just about to attempt a lift, they would be total concentration, total conviction to the lift, belief in himself, and professional pride. Until these qualities come together and crystallize, all the bells, buzzers, and gongs in the world can sound and Ron will not lift. Fortunately, he seems to have sufficient control over these manifestations of man against weight that the bar usually starts moving when there are about ten or less seconds to run. Again he takes another five years off my life while prolonging his own. With only 16 years difference between our ages, the bastard will obviously outlive as well as outlift me!

"In a contest, all he needs is a reassuring, familiar hand. He rises to the atmosphere generated by an audience but does not let it overpower him. He is very susceptible to people saying the wrong thing at the wrong time, and this just makes his job of concentration and conviction that bit harder. Ron is a very sensible lifter which is why he is consistent. Many lifters are good yet irresponsible and so have

INCLINE BENCH PRESSES with dumbbells are also a Collins favorite, particularly in the off-season at the first of every year.

many ups and downs. Ron is not irresponsible. *He does not fantasize.* He knows what he is capable of and is happier doing that than trying something for the sensationalism of it. To him, that's a cheap thrill; *success* is the real thrill.

"Although Ron's basic training does not alter a great deal, the last few weeks before a contest are really dedicated to conditioning the body *and* the mind for what is expected of them on the day of the contest and to convince himself that all the previous weeks' hard training has built the strength required this particular time around. To this end Ron has in the past employed a few interesting tactics such as jumping 120 pounds in the squat a couple of times (600 to 720) just in case warmups are timed incorrectly. However, these last few weeks see Ron doing less repetition work on the squat and more steady in the groove singles, not necessarily heavy ones. He continues his progressive work on the bench press and he moves for one night a week to another club that's cool and has a bar with real sharp knurling for that one big confi-

dence booster of a deadlift. Also, the last few weeks see him gradually reduce his bodybuilding movements so he may be that little bit sharper for the next heavy workout. There is no rule of thumb for these last weeks but these are the ideas that go through his mind.

"If there is a heavy wild week it will probably be week four or three before the meet. If there are failures then (which there seldom are) they will not be the downers that failures can be just before a contest. The last two weeks he plays very much by ear—nothing pushed, just accepted. The final week sees a hard workout Monday, and easy, light reps Wednesday, leaving out the deadlift. I think we have adopted this method because quite often when you reach big lifts (for example, Ron's 750 squat) in week four or three you say to yourself 'Where can you go from there?' So, instead of trying to go higher in the next couple of weeks, you accept lighter weights but make them easier, *thereby keeping the mind fresh and responsive for the big day*. It is more important to employ such training in the

THESE SEQUENCE PHOTOS by Jan Todd at the 1976 World Championships show Collins using a relatively flat back as he pulls a powerful 722 pounds. Note the official in the right of the pictures physically sympathizing with Ron by leaning back as the weight goes up.

squat than in the bench press, as the bench press can be worked right up to the last Wednesday. It's a far less variable lift.

"From being one of the people most keen on seeing a Ron Collins-Larry Pacifico clash I now have to concede that such a match would be a mistake. Both these lifters are peers in their sport and this could tarnish either or both of their careers. What I especially like about Ron and Larry is that they are neither one what I call 'freak' lifters. They use muscles and not gimmicks or styles to get the big poundages. Ron can squat as much with or without the tight suits and so can Larry, virtually. They both have been or are world squat record-holders without the natural leverages of a Marvin Phillips, George Crawford, or Inaba. They are both good, very good, deadlifters with good lockouts, normal length arms, and conventional style, and they are both good bench pressers, Larry qualifying also as exceptional.

"Put these thoughts and this background together and you come somewhere near to understanding why, at close to 43 years of age, Ron Collins is going to get stronger yet for years to come, while looking better physically than lifters half his age, including me."

Concerning the proposed Super Bowl between Ron and Larry Pacifico, Ron feels that at 181 Larry couldn't compete

effectively against him, and that at 198 he would have to train for a couple of years before all the extra weight would begin to really work for him. Suggestions have been made that they split the difference and meet one another at approximately 190 pounds, but this is impractical since it might conflict with either of their yearly training cycles. Should they work out the details and agree to a head-on match, it would be worth crawling through three miles of prickly pear to see.

An extremely calm and thoughtful man, as Tony pointed out, Ron works as an engineer. He's been with the same company for almost 20 years, and they are very understanding when he needs time off for his travels. His wife and son also support him strongly in what he does, and see that he gets the sort of food he needs to continue his remarkable career. Regarding diet, he tells me that he takes very little supplements other than vitamin C, but he eats lots of meat, fish, and the whites of eggs.

Through my years of Collins-watching, I've come to have a deep and abiding respect for this small but gallant man. Some of us in lifting tower over him by a foot or more, but he towers over all of us when it comes to that one crucial aspect of being a champion that Hemingway claimed was the most important. True champions, Papa said, have "*grace under pressure*." No one in lifting has this as Ron has it.

In closing, I'd like to quote several passages from an earlier article of mine. The passages, dealing with Collins' lifting in 1975 in the World Championships in England, seem to me to capture the unquenchable spirit of this man who burns with a cool blue fire.

At 622.75 (282.5 Kg.), Collins emerged to virtually ice down another world crown, and as he strode to the bar, his muscles bulging tightly under his fair skin, his modishly long, jet black hair surrounding his youthful face, no one would have guessed he was 41 years old. He hauled the 622.75 from the floor in a surge of strength that brought shouts of certain victory from the crowd, but the effort caused Collins to cramp badly, and the cramps, plus

the slight injury he apparently suffered in the squat, made it necessary for the spotter-loaders to carry him off the stage.

A few minutes later, Collins recovered well enough backstage to hobble back onto the platform to take a 672.5 (305 Kg.) second attempt which, if successful, would give him a new world record total. He limped out, chalking up as the crowd cheered him on, then bent, set, heaved, and the record was his, though again it caused him to cramp so badly that he could barely walk away. As he limped off, I'm sure that most people thought that the injury, the cramping, the new world-total record, and the world title would mean that he would forego his last attempt, but then Ron Collins does not think now, never has thought,

THE TWO GREATEST powerlifters in the world—Ron Collins and Larry Pacifico—on the morning after their successful defense of their respective world titles. As of this writing Ron has won five world titles and Larry has won six. They are the best of friends and have corresponded with and helped one another for years. *(Right)* When he squats, Collins leans well into the weight on the way up. Note that he uses a foot stance that is unusually narrow for a world-class powerlifter.

and never *will* think like 'most people'.

And so he asked for 700 pounds (317.5 Kg.) to be loaded onto the bar. To describe this dramatic attempt, I will quote exactly from my notes, as I wrote them that evening.

"He steps painfully onto the platform for the 700. I think he's got a shot at it. The crowd is shouting, helping to psyche him for the effort. He limps to the bar, pain showing on his face, but he is careful not to rush the lift. As he bends to grip the bar, he has only ten seconds left on the clock. He sets, looks up, pulls, and simply masters the weight, and as the weight goes up, so does the crowd, brought up by the awesome courage and tenacity of the man. And I, for the first time in my life, feel tears come unbidden to my eyes as I join in paying tribute to this man who has as much right as any man ever has to be called history's greatest powerlifter. The ability to make such a lift with only the pressure of pride driving away the pain moved me as I have never before been moved by a lift. Perhaps it's partly because in winning, he won for Great Britain, who had worked so hard and provided so well and generously to stage the contest. For them to have at long last a champion of their own seemed to redeem the British team and create a proper mood for this great meet."

In that contest, Ron was chosen Champion of Champions—Best Lifter, an honor he won again in 1976. If anyone ever deserved it more I've yet to see him. To me, that phrase serves better than any other could to describe this wonderful, ageless athlete. He is, indeed, powerlifting's Champion of Champions.

LARRY PACIFICO

When those of you who know him think of or hear about Larry Pacifico, what word or quality comes first to your mind? Strength? Consistency? Agility? Style? Thickness? Power? Moleness? Without question he is all of these: strong, consistent, agile, stylish, muscularly thick, powerful, and who could deny that when he weighed around 242 pounds and wore his dark glasses he looked for all the world like the famous character in Kenneth Grahame's *Wind in the Willows*, Mr. Mole? These days, although he no longer looks like Mr. Mole, having shed his shades and 44 pounds, he still possesses all the other qualities, and another one besides—one which to me characterizes Pacifico the lifter and Pacifico the man more accurately than any other possibly could. That quality is class.

I consider it a rare possession. Rigert has it. And John Grimek. And Sandow did. It has only incidentally to do with winning. You can win for years and never have it. It seems somehow less an attainment than a blessing, something given to a few by God or circumstance so that those of us who lack it can see it enfleshed and have it before us as a goal or a yardstick.

To be able to include in this section of my book a man who is so blessed is a real pleasure, because in planning the book I felt obligated to use whichever lifters were generally considered to be the best powerlifters in the world, and my choice—other than Jan, who *demanded* to be included—seemed to me to boil down to two men: Larry Pacifico and Ron Collins, both legendary, both loaded with class; so I was spared the difficulty of having to close this tribute to our sport with a chapter on some record-holding winner or other whose only class was his bodyweight. Larry began his lifting life after a

IN THIS CASE it's hard to tell whether the P he's wearing around his neck stands for Pacifico or Power-lifting. Winner of more world championships than anyone in history, Larry is respected by all who know him.

AT AGE 13 Larry was already interested in strength, but who could've guessed what he would become?

debilitating attack of rheumatic fever when his father prescribed "iron pills" in the form of a set of springs and a home-made cement barbell. Larry was then 11 years old, stood five feet tall and weighed 105 pounds. He continued to train off and on throughout high school, although his main energies in those years were spent on other competitive sports: base-ball, track and field, and gymnastics. His father was an avid baseball fan and dreamed the father's dream of having a son in the big leagues, but although he was a wonderful player, Larry realistically understood that at 5-feet 6-inches his chances of a major-league career were about as slim as Farrah Fawcett-Majors' bicep. So, out of a continuing desire to do something of which his father could be

proud—something for which Larry would, in his own words, "stand out in a crowd"—he turned away from team sports to the lonely passion of individual competition.

This turning led him to the New York State High School Championship on the still rings, and in track and field to the following outstanding performances: At a bodyweight of 165 pounds, Larry heaved the shot 57 feet, surely one of the greatest pound-for-pound puts ever made. In ad-dition, he spun the discus 164 feet, long jumped 22 feet 5 inches, ran the 100-yard dash in 10 seconds, and high jumped four feet, four inches over his own height.

After high school he began to concen-trate on his lifting, and, as his concentra-tion sharpened, his strength grew and grew again and his muscles spread and rose beneath his skin as he bade them to push, pull, and perform. And his father saw it and was proud. Larry's awesome capacity to fulfill his dreams continued as he went from strength to strength, win-ning contests and moving up in his career in the health-studio business until now, as this is being written, he is at the absolute peak of his athletic prime being on the verge of winning his seventh consecutive world title. In addition, he's well along toward almost certain big-time success in the gym business as the vice-president of the New Life Health Studios chain, demonstrating once again that given enough determination and capacity for self-discipline, a man can be successful in both lifting *and* a career, simultaneously.

How did he do it? To begin, besides the above mentioned qualities of determination and self-discipline, he found a routine that worked for him and he stuck with it. Allowing for occasional variations, this is how it goes, based on approximate training bests of a 730 squat, 550 bench, and 750 deadlift, at 208 bodyweight.

Monday

Deadlift

245 × 8	625 × 3
335 × 6	670 × 3
425 × 4	690 × 3
515 × 3	700 × 3

Situps

50

Tuesday

Squat

135 × 10	555 × 3
225 × 8	605 × 3
315 × 6	660 × 3
405 × 4	675 × 3
505 × 3	

Bench Press

135 × 10	505 × 3
225 × 8	505 × 3
315 × 6	505 × 3
405 × 4	405 × 8
485 × 3	405 × 8
505 × 3	

Situps

50

Wednesday

Power Clean

225 × 5	340 × 3
275 × 3	360 × 3
315 × 3	360 × 3

Shrugs (behind the legs)

405 × 10   405 × 10

Shrugs (in front)

475 × 10

THESE SEQUENCE PHOTOS by Jan Todd catch Larry as he fights from the bottom up through the sticking point.

Shrugs (behind)
475 × 10
Shrugs (in front)
475 × 10
Shrugs (behind)
475 × 10
Heavy Curl (5 sets, EZ Curl bar)
155 × 6
Curl Machine (close grip)
125 × 10 (5 sets)
Concentration Curl with dumbbell
50 × 8 (4 sets)
Triceps Press

110 × 10	200 × 4
160 × 8	225 × 3 (5 sets)
180 × 6	

Situps
50

Thursday
Off

Friday
same as Tuesday

Saturday
Lat-Machine Pulldown

120 × 10	160 × 10 (3 sets)

Dumbbell Row (one hand)
75 × 10 (5 sets)
Straight Arm Pullover (wide grip)
50 × 10 (4 sets)
Situps
50

Sunday
Squats and bench presses: Using the same system of repetitions but using a narrow-foot stance in the squat and a narrow grip in the bench press, and using between 60 percent and 70 percent of the poundages he uses in his Tuesday and Friday work-outs.
Situps
50. In addition, Larry skips rope and jogs a mile almost every day.

That's it. Not too complicated, just hard and heavy. For those of you who, like me, are interested in a man's all-time training bests, here are some of Larry's. At a bodyweight of 242, he made 635 in the bench press with elbow wraps and 610 without them. In addition, he squatted and deadlifted 780 pounds at that weight, both wrapless. He has curled 225 with his back against a wall, and he has done a single in the triceps extension with 330 pounds—down to his hips and back with an EZ curl bar. Of all his best feats, however, he is proudest of having gotten three reps with 315 in the strict, seated press behind the neck at a bodyweight of 238.

THIS PHOTO SHOWS the extremely narrow grip Larry was forced to use at the 1976 World Championships because of his injured shoulder. Even so, the 402.5 he made was more than enough to allow him to capture his sixth consecutive world crown.

AN EARLY PHOTO of Larry before he moved his grip out. When he *did* widen his hand spacing, his bench press increased almost immediately to 500.

In preparation for this chapter, I asked him what advice he would give to a teenager who was just beginning as a powerlifter. He said,

In my view, a beginner should stick with sets of eight and ten with a comfortable weight trying limits only once a month. He should avoid full squats at the very beginning of his training, but should do partial squats so that every month he works into a slightly lower position until the legal depth is reached. Another thing to avoid is trying to ride the bar too far down the back in the squat. Wait till the trapezius muscles have begun to develop so the bar will have a solid, comfortable place to rest. Also, don't begin with heavy lying triceps presses; stick to close-grip benches for a year or so till the tendons toughen. In fact, I'd advise any beginner to start on a fairly standard routine for the first year and then, if the desire is there, start piling on that heavy iron.

Concerning the much talked about summit confrontation in the 198-pound class between himself and England's Ron Collins, Larry had this to say:

I talked to Tony Fitton the other day and he said Ron has had second thoughts about this showdown. Tony said that because of the recent lifting of Dennis Wright and Walter Thomas, Ron wants to stay in the 181's and put the total up a little higher. It sounds to me as if he wants to postpone the showdown until 1978 and that's fine with me. I want to win the 220's again this year at the World's to go with the other midheavy wins I've had. This would give me two world titles in the 198's, three in the 220's and two in the 242's. After that plus the extra year to promote it, we can have the showdown.

One thing is certain—time is on Pacifico's side as he's 13 years younger than Collins and his progress has been steady since he began competing. In support of this statement I offer the following list of all the contests in which he has ever lifted, along with the poundages he registered.

CONCENTRATING AND THEN pulling the weight he needed to ice down the 198.25-pound class in the 1976 World Championships.

*Best Lifter Award   +World Record   #World Championships

Date	Bench Press	Squat	Deadlift	Total	Bodyweight
4-66	350	415	500	1265	176
5-66	355	415	505	1275	178
11-66	370	425	525	1320	181
4-67	385	425	530	1340	180*
4-67	390	445	530	1365	181*
5-67	390	450	520	1360	179
8-67	375	430	550	1355	180
8-67	375	440	550	1365	181
9-67	395	450	560	1405	180*
2-68	350	460	575	1385	181*
3-68	375	450	505	1330	180
4-68	375	470	580	1425	181*
5-68	390	480	580	1450	180*
5-68	400	485	585	1470	181*
6-68	390	465	550	1405	180
8-68	375	470	570	1415	181
12-68	440	540	620	1600	193*
2-69	430	530	600	1560	194*
3-69	420	570	575	1565	194*
4-69	450	605	620	1675+	197*
7-69	460	610	630	1700+	198*
9-69	455	580	620	1655	198
11-69	450	550	600	1600	199
12-69	460	600	605	1665	198*
3-70	455	620	630	1705	198*
4-70	465	625	660	1750+	198*
6-70	465	655	635	1755+	198*
9-70	455	660	645	1760+	198
11-70	500	700	665	1865	221*
2-71	465	600	600	1665	197*
4-71	480	640	650	1770+	198*
5-71	500+	650	665	1815+	198*
9-71	510+	625	670	1805	198
11-71	515+	625	660	1800	198*#
2-72	505	635	640	1780	198
3-72	515+	650	670	1835+	198*
4-72	530‡	655	715	1900‡	198*
6-72	575+	700	650	1925	230*
10-72	560	710	705	1975	224*
11-72	575+	700	700	1975	226#
3-73	580+	720	730	2030	231*
5-73	540+	700+	670	1910+	220*
7-73	590+	750+	740	2080+	237*
11-73	550	750+	705	2005	242*#

3–74	560+	710+	730	2000+	220*
4–74	545	730+	730	2005+	220*
11–74	570+	705	680	1955	219#
5–75	545	760+	715+	2020+	220*
9–75	555	710	735+	2000	220*
11–75	551½	650¼	705½	1907	218#
4–76	530+	685	720	1935+	198*
8–76	505	680	715	1900	198*
11–76	407	690	705	1802	198#

47 World Records
53 Contests
5 Losses
35 Best Lifter Awards
1969 Junior National Champion
1970, 1971, 1975, 1976 Senior National Champion
1971, 1972, 1973, 1974, 1975, 1976 World Champion

A bed of roses, though, it hasn't been. During Larry's training for the 1976 World Championships, he sustained a serious injury to his left shoulder, so serious that he felt he would be unable to compete. Late one night he called me and told me of his pain and his sadness and asked me for my advice. He said that it was completely impossible for him to train at all on the bench press, but that he felt that he might have a chance to score highly enough on the squat and deadlift in the meet that all he would need in the bench to win would be a little over 300 pounds, a lift that he figured he could make no matter *how* much his shoulder hurt.

When he asked me what I thought, I said, "Larry, do you think you could get between 300 and 350 and not hurt your shoulder any worse than it's hurt now?" He said he believed he could, but that he was worried because he didn't want to disappoint his fans and because just about everyone he'd asked had urged him to withdraw from the coming competition. Then he said softly, "But I want to lift, Doc, I want to lift." I told him that if

he were a young lifter just beginning his career or a lifter who was training to defend a local championship, I'd recommend that he play it safe and withdraw. Then I went on to say, "But that's not my advice to you, Mole. You've won five titles in a row. I think you ought to go get that sixth."

And so, a month or so later, when the smoke had cleared after the 1976 World's, I was pleased to be able to write the following account of what took place.

The 198.25-pound class:
Speaking of Larry Pacifico, it should be noted that the fact that he lifted at all bears witness to his enormous love of powerlifting, for he was hurt—badly hurt—in the left shoulder and knew that to lift was not only to suffer pain but to risk further, and perhaps permanent, injury. But lift he did, accepting the pain and the risk, to defend his world championship for the fifth consecutive time. (Twice he's been champ as a 198, twice as a 220, and twice as a 242).

IN TRAINING, LARRY takes his normal grip with 455 pounds. *(Right)* Larry can deadlift almost exactly the same weight with this sumo-style deadlift as with the regular style.

He squatted well, handling 689.25 solidly but losing 705.25 on balance. In the bench, he asked the spotters to place the bar on his chest, from which position he was able to tuck his arms against his sides with his elbows raised, thus allowing him to half bench, half tricep press the weight. He began with 352.5, which shot up quickly but hurt so badly that he wanted to quit. However, he was somewhat worried about England's Eamon Toal, so he waited until Toal opened with 402.25 before deciding that to be on the safe side he should try to match this weight. Though still forced to use the half tricep press style, he is so unbelievably strong and tough that he was able to lift the bar and hold it for the clap and as he did so the crowd stood and cheered for Larry as he got up slowly from the bench, his left arm held tightly against his side as his face twisted with the pain.

In the deadlift, he opened strongly with 644.75 to clinch his sixth

world's, then went on to make a powerful 705.25 before failing with an anticlimactic 727.5. After he finished on stage, he came to sit with me and as he sat down he looked over and smiled and said, "You know what, Doc? It hurt like hell but it was worth it. It was worth every bit of it."

Following the World's, Larry underwent major surgery to repair the injured shoulder and after a lengthy and confidence-wilting recovery period, he seems to be headed back to the top. His bench is up to 500 and climbing and the pain is gone; so I guess that the rest of the 198-pounders in the upcoming National and World Championships will have to once again forget about first and try for the silver.

It seems that, at least for now, Larry has no plans for retirement. When I asked him about his goals as a lifter, he replied that his only goal was to improve. "As long as I continue to improve, I'll continue to lift. In the past, particularly after the death of my father a few years ago, I seriously considered retiring and even at one point decided to retire, but after talking to you in Chattanooga, I began to see that since I still enjoyed training and competing, there was no real reason to quit. For me this was a turning point. I plan to lift as much as I can for as long as I can."

What better answer could there be? "As much as I can for as long as I can." Once, writing in *Muscular Development*, I announced, at his request, his retirement. It saddened me to have to do it, and I spoke to him later not only of my sense of loss but of the sense of loss that I felt would later come to him. I paraphrased the Beatles, saying, "The lifts you give are equal to the lifts you take." And so the King came back, and remains, lighting up the platforms of the world with his electrifying strength, ably representing other lifters in his capacity as a voting member of the National Powerlifting Committee, writing to lifters everywhere with advice and encouragement, and, in general, adding something of which our new sport has great and continuing need—a touch of class. Long lift the King.

AN EXCELLENT GYMNAST, Larry often does handstand press-ups as an assistance exercise for his bench press. Note the muscles. *(Lower left)* Larry is a firm believer in the value of the shoulder shrug, and he does them both in front of and behind the body. *(Right)* Power cleans are one of Larry's favorite exercises.

JAN TODD

It all began with an untossed caber, in a meadow by a Georgia millpond. An "untossed caber?" Well . . . actually, "caber" is the term used to describe a long slender log, rather like a small telephone pole, which characterizes one of the athletic events in the Scottish Highland Games. The idea of the event, after you have stood the caber on end and picked it up so that the bottom end is cradled in your hands and balanced against your chest, is to run forward several steps, allowing the top end of the caber to overbalance forward and then, just as it is falling, to thrust upward with your legs and arms so that the caber is flipped, or "tossed," end over end.

JAN TODD TRAINING at the Powerbuilder's Gym in Macon, Georgia, just before breaking the world deadlift record for women which had stood for almost 50 years.

A perfect toss results in the caber landing so that the end you had in your hands points away from you in the exact direction you intended to toss it. Imagine a huge clock face, with you and the untossed caber in the center. Your aim is to run slowly toward the "twelve" and flip the caber over once so that the end you were holding lands pointing at the center of the number 12. A "one o'clock" or "eleven o'clock" toss are both better than a "two o'clock" or "ten o'clock" toss and

so on. A truly heavy caber is difficult to turn over at all; what usually happens is that the end in your hands never "turns," but falls back to the ground so that it points *at* you rather than *away* from you.

What happened in the meadow that spring afternoon had to do with the fact that a bunch of people—teachers and students who played on a Mercer University intramural softball team—were having an end-of-the-season party out at my place. During the course of the party, a few of us wound up sitting on a pile of logs which I had stacked in the meadow after having cleaned up the damage of a winter ice storm; we were having a beer and talking when somehow caber tossing was mentioned. After that, of course, nothing would do but to give it a try, and within a couple of minutes a log had been selected which was heavy enough to be a challenge but light enough to be turned by at least some of the team members and assorted hangers-on.

THE MUSCLES OF Jan's back and neck stretch as she finishes the 394.5-pound deadlift and breaks the world record which had stood for 48 years.

It so happened that the folks who began tossing or trying to toss the caber were all men, mostly faculty, and it further happened that of the four who first tried it, all but one could turn the caber over and make it land so that it pointed somewhere near high noon. The one who failed was a professor of philosophy, a man to whom happiness was never having to admit he was sorry. The fact that at that time he jogged every day come hell or high water added to the old red-neck pleasure the rest of us took from watching him wobble forward with the caber and heave it, only to have the end slow down, stop, then fall back to the ground where it lay pointing at him accusingly.

By the time he'd tried and failed five or six times, a small crowd was gathering and comments of "Oh, no, he can't get it up!" were sending whoops of laughter skittering across the millpond. And then, as he paused for breath and composure, a young woman—a student, in fact, in the philosophy department—came down off the hill, stepped right up there and stood the caber on end, lifted it, took a few steps forward, and turned it a flip which would have brought a smile to the face of the most dour Scot, landing it so that it pointed dead straight, to the delighted, and sustained, cheers of the crowd.

As near as I can tell, that was the day I began to love her. I had always been taken by her energy and her skill at athletics, but there was something in the way she stepped up to that log and lifted it— no giggling, no false modestness—that I must admit I truly admired. Still do.

Her name was Jan Suffolk and a year or so later we were married. I was teaching and she was working and taking a few courses in graduate school, but neither of us was doing much in the way of sports other than the weekly workout I put in at the tiny Mercer weight room, when one day she came down with me and I showed her a few of the things that women do at the better-equipped health spas across the country: posture-building and figure-shaping exercises with light barbells and dumbbells.

She seemed to enjoy the workout and soon she was going every week. Then, under her urging, we began to train twice a week, something I hadn't done since retiring from competitive lifting six or seven years before. She worked hard with the weights, as she did with everything, but never extended herself as far as maximum weights were concerned. Always naturally strong and fast, she used weight training as a way to stay fit rather than as a way to dramatically increase her strength.

On a Christmas trip to my home in Texas in 1973, however, she saw something which changed her mind about heavy weights. We were down at a fine old place called the Texas Athletic Club, taking a big dose of the iron pills, when a young woman walked in and began to train. She started with the deadlift, which is done by simply walking up to the barbell, gripping it with both hands, and then lifting it upward slowly until you are standing upright with your arms and legs straight and the bar resting against the front of your thighs. Although small, the young woman was amazingly strong and she kept putting extra weights on the ends of the bar after each deadlift until she reached her limit at 225 pounds, over 100 pounds more than she weighed.

When the young woman finished deadlifting, Jan and I talked to her and found out that she always trained heavy and had, as a matter of fact, placed third in the bantamweight class in a recent "men's" contest. She said the heavier weights she lifted had simply made her stronger and had not made her overly muscular or larger. By far the most convincing argument was her graceful car-

JAN DRIVES UP out of a 385 squat during a training session at the Texas Athletic Club in Austin during the spring of 1977. Notice how closely she's being spotted by her husband and Robert Young. It pays to be safe.

riage and her handsome body, which was neither slender nor stocky but was, to me, rather like Baby Bear's porridge. As I resumed my workout, she and Jan continued to talk, and in a few minutes I noticed that Jan was deadlifting, first with light weights and then with heavier ones until she matched the other young woman with a deadlift of 225 pounds. On

WHILE IN TEXAS, Jan sought the advice of world 242-pound champion Doug Young, long one of her strongest (not to mention biggest) supporters.

the way home, Jan and I talked about strength, and size, and womanhood, and I told her about some of the famous strongwomen of the vaudeville and circus days.

I told her about Kate Sandwina, the phenomenal German woman who was a center ring attraction for years with the Ringling Brothers' Circus in the early part of this century. I told her how the 6-feet 1-inch, 210-pound Sandwina juggled Max, her 160-pound husband, as part of her show and how she was so strong she had continued doing her circus act, which included carrying a 600-pound cannon across the ring on one shoulder up until the day she bore a son and how she then rested, like God, for a day after her labors before she went back into the center ring, grabbed old Max and went to juggling.

I told her as well about the recent research out in California which had demonstrated that women, when size and muscle weight (as opposed to excess, or fatty, weight) are taken into consideration, appear to be stronger than men in their legs and hips. And when we got back to my parents' home, I dug out some of my old magazines and books and showed her pictures and stories about some of the few women who through the years have trained with heavy weights. While we were looking through all this marvelous old stuff, we came across a page from the *Guinness Book of World Records* which stated that Mlle. Jane de Vesley of France had made the highest authenticated deadlift on record for a woman (392 pounds) way back in 1926. As she read this page, Jan paused for a minute, looked over at me, and said with a barely controlled smile, "I think I can beat that." I sort of figured she could too, and so when we went back to Georgia we outlined a program which was designed to build a foundation of overall strength sufficient to enable her to exceed the 392-pound world record. The two basic exercises we chose were the squat and, of course, the deadlift itself. In addition, exercises such as the bench press were included so that her upper body would also become strong, thus avoiding a disproportionate increase in strength. We scheduled two workouts per week with the weights, each one lasting one and one-half to two hours. Finally, we planned to run a mile or so and do a few wind sprints on a couple of our off-days each week.

We were fortunate to be able to train at a thoroughly equipped gym in downtown Macon called Powerbuilders because there weren't sufficient weights or space in the dark and dismal little basement hole in the wall where the weights were kept at Mercer. The owner of Powerbuilders took the enlightened position that although his was a gym for men and not a men's and women's health spa (with separate locker-room, shower, and rest-room facilities for women) if Jan didn't mind training with the men and dressing elsewhere he would be glad to have her. As it turned out, having her was a good

WARMING UP WITH 315 in the deadlift, Jan went on up that day to a high of 435, a weight no other woman has even approached.

thing for the young men who trained there because they were forced by Jan's growing strength to look to their own improvement, and they were forced by her relatively small size to unlearn some of the legends that abound about women and weight lifting.

But the thing that amazed us both as we worked out at Powerbuilders was the way in which she was treated by the other members. We had *expected* that the average high school or college age weight trainer wouldn't like to be outlifted "by a girl" and would stop just short of herniation to keep from having it happen, but we had not expected the warmth with which she was taken in and accepted as being simply another person who was serious about training and who deserved the same attention, help, and encouragement as anyone else.

And so with a goal in mind and ideal training conditions, Jan began to close the gap on Mlle. de Vesley's 48-year-old record. By February, she had done 295 pounds; by March, 315; and by April, 325. But then in May, just after having made an easy 335, she injured her back while plowing up our garden out at the Millhouse and was forced to discontinue her heavy training until the following fall—the fall of 1974. We waited until her back was thoroughly healed before beginning again with the big weights, but by late October she was ready to go. Rather quickly she moved past her best of the previous spring and, by Christmas, surrounded and encouraged by all the wonderful old rowdies at the Texas Athletic Club, she made 370.

After returning to Georgia, we began to look around for a lifting contest so that she would have a certain day toward which to train and on which to "peak," and so that whatever she lifted would be judged by nationally certified referees and thus be "official" or at least official enough for the purposes of breaking the record. Finally, although we would have preferred an earlier meet, we decided to shoot for an upcoming contest which was to be held in Chattanooga, Tennessee, on May 3. The problem with a meet almost four months in the future is that it's very hard to train that long without losing your edge and going stale. Athletes such as swimmers, track and field people, and cyclists all experience this, and hindsight makes it clear that she should have taken a short layoff in January and then worked back into top shape by the first of May.

One of the hardest things in the world for an athlete to do, however, is to take a voluntary layoff just when things are really going well, and so she continued to train. And sure enough, she went stale in February and her improvements stopped completely. And in March she actually began to lose a little ground. Finally, in April, mainly through an enormous effort of will, she began to put those few vital pounds back on her lifts, and a week and a half before the meet, she deadlifted 385,

less than ten pounds away from the record. Ten pounds, however, is ten pounds, and the higher you go the harder they come; so as we drove into Chattanooga on the Friday night before the lifting, we were counting on the adrenalized excitement of the contest itself to provide the few extra pounds she would need.

LIFTING IN NEWFOUNDLAND on June 4, 1977, Jan opened her assault on the women's world records with an easy first attempt squat of 369.5. She went on to a total 1,042. (Below) How could she miss that heavy squat after having her knees wrapped by her husband, former world champion, and Doug Young, current world champion?

On the day of the meet the sports section of the Chattanooga newspaper had a big story about Jan's assault on the old record. The local television stations also covered it, and so the spring was tightening down as the time to lift approached. And then finally, at long, long last, after all those months of narrowly focused attention and plain hard work, it was time. All the bait had been cut—it was time to fish.

She was given a special spot on the evening's program, and so she warmed up backstage during the minutes before she was to make the attempt by loosening up and starting with 135, then going in turn to 225, 275, and 315. It was her intention to take her last heavy warm-up with 355 onstage as it would give her a chance to test not only herself but the bar and the audience as well. And so the big Olympic bar was loaded to 355 pounds, and she moved onto the stage to a huge ovation. Surprised, she hurriedly "chalked" her hands to assist her grip, walked up to the bar, and successfully lifted it. Again the audience cheered, but the lift hadn't been as easy as I had hoped, and so as she rested and psyched herself for the 395, I was worried that she might feel disheartened and thus lose the confidence without which record weights simply cannot be achieved.

But I kept my worry to myself as I handed her the block of chalk because I'd been down the road she was now on a few times myself and I knew that from now on it was hers to do. And then she was ready. She finished chalking her hands and turned to me with a look I have seen a few times before in world-class competition—a look through the flat, emotionless eyes of those who are far, far into themselves, walking where no foot-

HER FACE AND eyes showing the strain of the lift, Jan prepares to replace the bar on the racks after making a three-white-light success with the world record weight of 424.5.

steps are. Then she went out to the applause and shouts of the crowd, bent down, gripped the bar, got set, and began to pull. Slowly, the bar broke free from the ground and she fought it to her knees where it slowed, almost stopping, but as the crowd stood and screamed she kept on tugging and the bar moved past her knees and, inch by slow inch, it slid up her thighs until her head was back, her shoulders were straight and the record was hers.

It was a beautiful, limit lift, heartstopping in its slowness, and the judges gladly signed the necessary papers so that the verification could be submitted to the *Guinness Book*. And the following fall, the new edition of *Guinness* had an item on Page 335 which read:

The highest competitive two-handed deadlift by a woman is 394.5 lb.

(178.9 Kg.) by Jan Suffolk Todd (U.S.) at Chattanooga, Tennessee, on 3 May 1975.

Since that time, Jan has continued to train, at first simply concentrating on the deadlift but later, during the past six months, working hard on all three of the powerlifts. After taking the summer off in 1975 to help me work our farm and to get ready for our move to Nova Scotia, she began going in with me in the fall to work out at the weight room at Dalhousie University, where I teach. Once again we were fortunate enough to find good training partners who took Jan's lifting seriously and training facilities which had at least the bare essentials (Olympic weights, squat rack, and bench), so her strength continued to improve.

By Christmas time she was back up to almost 400 pounds in the deadlift, but on the day after Christmas she slipped on

SO NEAR AND yet so far. Jan struggles unsuccessfully to finish a 445-pound deadlift in the first national powerlifting championships for women in April of 1977 in Nashua, New Hampshire. Had she completed the lift, she would have added a 1,000 pound total to her first place finish, but the lift wouldn't quite go.

some icy steps at a friend's farm and suffered a severe ankle sprain. Even though she wasn't able to run freely on the bad ankle for over a year, she started training early in January and did what she could with her limited flexibility. She was particularly hampered in the squat, and, to a lesser but still serious extent, in the bottom part of the deadlift, but she kept pushing and her power began to return. By April she was ready for another world-record attempt, and so she went to a contest up in Sydney, here in Nova Scotia, and pulled a powerful 412.5.

HERE SHE IS masquerading as the All-American girl next door. This is the photo which appeared in *Sports Illustrated* following her 1,042 total.

As she had done the year before, she eased off during the summer and worked with me on our new farm. Then in the fall she began teaching at the nearby high school, and with the help of a large group of interested friends and students, she was able to raise enough money to buy a 600-pound Olympic set, a lifting platform, a competition-style bench, and a sturdy set of squat racks. Finally, just before Christmas, she had gotten the 50 or 60 students (half boys and half girls) well enough acquainted with the basics that she was able to give a few thoughts to her own training and she decided that, since her ankle was almost completely healed, she would concentrate on all three lifts—rather than just the deadlift—for the first time in her life.

A national women's contest, scheduled for April 17, was then in the planning stages, and so she organized her training so that she would hopefully "peak" on the day of the meet. And as she began to bear down on the squat, she made such tremendous gains that she realized that by April 17 she might have an outside shot at becoming the first woman to total 1,000 pounds on the three powerlifts. And she damn near made it, too, winning the meet and reaching 970 via a 385 squat, a 170 bench press, and a 415 deadlift. Twice she tried 445 pounds in an effort to make the half-ton total, but although she came within inches each time of pulling it, she failed.

FROM TIME TO time Jan has included snatches in her routine. She is shown here doing repetitions with 135.

And the failure, for her, outweighed the fact that her 385 squat, 415 deadlift, and 970 total were more than any woman had ever made in competition. The "failure" was bitter to her because she knew from her training that she was *ready* to do a thousand. When we got back home after the meet she told me that she'd decided to not take a layoff, as she'd planned to do, but to keep applying the pressure until June 4, the day on which a contest was scheduled up in Newfoundland. She was determined to reach the goal she'd set for herself, and she was willing, as were all the other wonderful athletes in this book, to pay the price of the ticket to get there.

One of the most difficult things in powerlifting or any other similar sport is to train for months toward a contest, carefully pyramiding your workouts to peak on the day of the meet, and then, instead of taking the usual obligatory post-contest layoff, to *extend* the peak and even *increase* it. But that's exactly what Jan decided to do and that's exactly what she did. On June 4—three days ago as I write this—she had one of those rare days when everything goes right and she made a 424.4-pound squat, a 176.4-pound bench press, and a 440.9-pound deadlift for a grand—really grand—total of 1,041.8 pounds, which is approximately 100 pounds more than any other woman has ever lifted. In order to best describe the routine she used to make these records, I've decided to simply list her complete program for the three weeks before the contest. In this way, her entire contest preparation can best be understood.

Sunday, May 15

Squat

135 × 8	355 × 2
205 × 5	380 × 2
265 × 3	400 × 1
295 × 3	415 × 1
325 × 2	

Bench Press

95 × 8	165 × 1
115 × 5	175 × 1
135 × 2	165 × 1
155 × 1	135 × 8

Deadlift

135 × 8	335 × 3
205 × 5	375 × 1
275 × 3	415 × 1

Deadlift

(pulled above knees but failed)

445

Wednesday, May 18

Squat

135 × 8	315 × 5
205 × 5	345 × 5

Bench Press

95 × 8	145 × 5
115 × 5	145 × 5
135 × 5	145 × 5

Bent Forward Row

135 × 6	185 × 6
155 × 6	195 × 6
175 × 6	205 × 6

Curl

30 × 10	50 × 10
40 × 10	60 × 10

Triceps Press

30 × 10	60 × 10
40 × 10	60 × 10

⎫ alternating sets ⎬

Sit-ups

3 sets of 20

JAN STANDS NEXT to 5'9" 230-lb. John Huble.

Friday, May 20

Narrow-Grip
  Bench Press
  45 × 8   125 × 5
  95 × 8   125 × 5
115 × 5

Curl
30 × 10   50 × 10
40 × 10   60 × 10   } alternating sets
Triceps Press
30 × 10   50 × 10
40 × 10
Sit-ups
3 sets of 25

Sunday, May 22

Squat
135 × 8   325 × 2
205 × 5   355 × 2
265 × 3   380 × 1
295 × 3   400 × 1
Bench Press
 95 × 8   165 × 1
115 × 5   175 × 1
135 × 3   135 × 8
155 × 1
Deadlift
135 × 8   385 × 1
225 × 5   425 × 1
295 × 3   445 × 1
345 × 2

Wednesday, May 25

Squat
135 × 9   320 × 5
205 × 5   350 × 5
280 × 5
Bench Press
 95 × 8   150 × 4
115 × 5   150 × 5
135 × 5   150 × 5
Bent Forward Row
135 × 6   185 × 5
155 × 6   195 × 5
175 × 10   40 × 10

Curl
20 × 10   40 × 10
30 × 10   40 × 10   } alternating sets
Triceps Press
20 × 10   40 × 10
30 × 10   40 × 10
Sit-ups
3 sets of 20

Friday, May 27

Narrow-Grip
  Bench Press
 95 × 6   125 × 5
115 × 5   125 × 5
125 × 5
Curl
20 × 10   40 × 10
40 × 10   } alternating sets
Triceps Press
20 × 10   40 × 10
40 × 10
Sit-ups
3 sets of 20

JAN AND CINDY Reinhoudt, the two strongest and best known women in powerlifting, following their appearance in Chattanooga in 1974.

Sunday, May 29

Squat
135 × 9   325 × 1
205 × 5   355 × 1
265 × 2   380 × 1
295 × 2

Bench Press

95 × 8	165 × 1
115 × 5	175 × 1
135 × 3	135 × 7
155 × 1	

Wednesday, June 1

Squat

Several sets of "free" squats

135 × 5	255 × 5
205 × 5	

Narrow-Grip Bench Press

95 × 5	115 × 5
115 × 5	

Bent Forward Row

135 × 4	175 × 4
155 × 4	

Curl

20 × 10	30 × 10

Triceps Press

20 × 10	30 × 10

} alternating sets

June 4, 1977, Contest Day

Squat

Several sets of "free" squats

135 × 8	369.4 × 1*
225 × 4	402.4 × 1*
295 × 2	424.4 × 1*
335 × 1	

Bench Press

95 × 8	165.4 ×1*
125 × 3	176.4 × 1*
145 × 1	

Deadlift

135 × 5	355 × 1
225 × 2	402.4 × 1*
315 × 2	440.9 × 1*

* Official attempt

Quite often, as one might suspect, she is asked why she trains and what she gets from lifting. We've talked about it quite a bit, and she seems to feel about it as I do. Neither of us have ever cared for the image of the "weak" woman. Jan was always a good runner and swimmer and player of games, and I grew up with a younger sister who was more than a match for most of the boys her age in the neighborhood in any contest of strength or skill. But the old myths die hard. Some people still preach that weakness is an aspect of femininity—that there is an iniquity in muscle itself, that there is a virtue in weakness, and a kind of assertive insolence in vigorous health. Preach on, we say, preach on, though the pews, praise God, are emptying.

Meanwhile, Jan plans to keep on lifting, teaching through her life that you don't have to be weak to be a woman. Every time she shoulders a 100-pound sack of corn at the feedstore, every time she carries a bag of groceries under each arm, every time she lifts our 150-pound mastiff into the back of the pickup, every time she helps our neighbors do some logging, every time she changes a tire, and every time she goes to the gym and trains, she chips away a little more of the wall of prejudice that has denied so many women access for so long to a crucial aspect of their human heritage, the aspect of strength. A wise and civilized nation should be concerned with helping men *and* women to attain the strength to endure and the skill to live not only in their bodies but through them. It takes strength to be gentle and compassionate, strength to love and be free. These are not, I know, scientific objectives, but they do seem to be worthwhile.

AT THE END of another workout, the Todds have to smile at the thought of heading home, making a fire in the woodstove, and having about two pounds apiece of blood-rare beefsteak. From time to time, life ain't bad.

appendix

Rules of the
International Powerlifting
Federation

A. Technical Rules:

1. The International Powerlifting Federation recognizes the following lifts and registers World Records of the same. The lifts contested are: (a) Deep Knee Bend or Squat; (b) Bench Press; and the (c) Deadlift.

2. Competition in open or team powerlifting shall be restricted to competitors 16 years of age or older.

3. A Junior lifter is one who is below the age of 20. On the day of his 20th birthday, he becomes a Senior.

4. The use of oil, grease, and all other lubricants is strictly prohibited. Powder only may be used.

5. Lifters must appear in correct and tidy dress which may consist of a vest with short sleeves and must consist of a full length lifting suit of stretch material, with an athletic supporter. Lifting suit straps shall be worn over the shoulders at all times while lifting.

6. Proper lifting costume shall include shoes. The height of the heel shall not be more than 4 cm. measured from the front of the heel. The heel must not extend laterally.

7. If a competitor wears a belt, it shall be a leather belt, not more than 10 cm. at its greatest width, and with a thickness not exceeding 13 mm. It shall have no additional padding, bracing, or supports, either interior or exterior. Its only nonleather entity shall be its buckle and attaching studs or stitching. It shall be worn around the waist.

8. The only badges or emblems to be worn on the lifter's costume in International competition are those of his country or national association.

9. Bandages:
   a. Rubber—Bandages of rubber or supports of rubber or rubber substitutes are forbidden.
   b. Wrist—Bandages of gauze or medical crepe with a maximum width of 8 cm. and a maximum length of one meter may be worn.
   c. Knee—Bandages of gauze or medical crepe may be worn with a maximum width of 8 cm. and a maximum length of two meters. Alternatively, an elastic knee cap may be worn with a maximum length of 20 cm. A combination of the two is forbidden.
   d. Body—Bandages around the torso are forbidden. Spot plasters to muscle injuries may be applied by the official IPF doctor on duty.
   e. Hands—Plasters on the fingers or inside of the hands are forbidden. If there are injuries to the hand, plasters may be applied by the official doctor on duty. If a strip is applied to the inside of the hand, it must not continue around the back of the hand.

f. Thumbs—Plasters may be worn on the thumbs, but shall not exceed two layers. Cloth or gauze bandages must not be worn on the thumbs.

g. Elbows—Bandages of any form on elbows are forbidden. The IPF doctor on duty must immediately inform the chief referee and the president of the jury which lifters have been given additional plasters.

h. If a lifter, after the referee's inspection, changes part of his costume, belt, or bandages or puts on anything which has not been authorized or which is contrary to the rules, he shall immediately be disqualified from the competition.

10. The following are correct dimensions of the bar and discs.
    a. Distance between collars: 1 m. 31 cm. at a maximum.
    b. Total length outside the sleeves: 2 m. 20 cm. at a maximum.
    c. Diameter of the bar: 28 mm. minimum; 29 mm. maximum.
    d. Diameter of the largest disc: 45 cm.
    e. Weight of the largest disc: 45 kg.
    f. Weight of the largest bar and collars: 25 kg.
    g. The discs must be in the following range: 45 kg., 25 kg., 20 kg., 15 kg., 10 kg., 5 kg., 2.5 kg., 1.25 kg.
    h. For record purposes, smaller discs may be added to the bar on a fourth attempt to give a weight of at least ½ kg. more than the existing world record.
    i. The color of the 20 kg. plates shall be blue. The color of the 25 kg. plates shall be red, and the 45 kg. plates shall be gold.

11. For all powerlifting contests organized under the rules of the IPF, only disc barbells are authorized. The use of short bars or ordinary weight will invalidate the contest. World records broken with equipment whose weights or dimensions are less or greater than those prescribed by the technical rules cannot be ratified.

12. A lift must be declared NO LIFT and the lifter may be disqualified if the weights are dropped intentionally.

13. Before the beginning of competitions, the recognized officials must check the weight of the bar and discs so that the total weight may be identical with that announced. All discs must have a clear indication of their weight.

14. Any lifter succeeding in an attempt for a world record will present himself immediately after the lift backstage for inspection for illegal wraps and clothing. The inspection is to be done by the three referees of the bodyweight class competing, before the meet continues. If he has illegal wraps or clothing, the lift shall be declared invalid and the lifter must be disqualified.

B. Categories of Weight Classes

There are ten categories of competition at world championships and regional games and those of a particular continent. Each country is allowed a maximum of ten competitors spread over the different categories, with a maximum of two lifters per category.

Example: A country may have one flyweight, one bantamweight, one featherweight, two middleweights, two lightheavyweights, one middleheavyweight, and two heavyweights. Replacements are optional. Two alternates are allowed. There are ten categories of competition:

Flyweight: up to 52 kg.
Bantamweight: up to 56 kg.
Featherweight: up to 60 kg.
Lightweight: up to 67.5 kg.
Middleweight: up to 75 kg.
Lightheavyweight: up to 82.5 kg.
Middleheavyweight: up to 90 kg.
100 Kilo class: up to 100 kg.
Heavyweight: up to 110 kg.
Superheavyweight: over 110 kg.

C. Weighing In

1. Weighing in of competitors must take place obligatorily one hour and 15 minutes before the beginning of the competition for a particular category. All the lifters in the category must attend the weigh-in, which shall be carried out in the presence of the three referees appointed for the category.

2. Weighing in will be in secret and the lifters will be allowed in one at a time. The weigh-in room will be locked and the persons allowed in it are the referees for the bodyweight class, the lifter, and his coach or trainer. The weigh-in results will not be made known until after the total weigh-in is finished.

3. Lifters shall be weighed nude. This shall apply along with all other rules regardless of the sex of the lifter and with no change in weigh-in circumstances. One of the three referees shall measure the belts and shoes and inspect the costumes and bandages of the lifters and shall record the details on the referees inspection form. All items to be worn by the lifter must be approved and marked accordingly. The assigned official shall see that the items worn during lifting correspond directly with the details on the inspection form. Lots shall be drawn to determine the order of weigh-in sequence. Once established, this order shall continue throughout the lifting.

4. Each competitor can only be weighed once. Only those greater or lighter than the category limit are allowed to return to the scales. They are allowed one hour at a maximum from the beginning of the weigh-in session to make the proper weight. After this time they will be eliminated.

5. A lifter who is too heavy may move into the next higher category if not more than one lifter from his country or team is entered in this category and provided that he has accomplished the required minimum qualifying total in this category.

6. When a lifter enters a weight class, for example the middleweight division, and for whatever reason fails to weigh as much as the lower limit of that class, he may drop into the lightweight division, provided he has the sufficient qualifying total required and that total was achieved in the lightweight class. A total achieved in the middleweight division will not fulfill the requirements.

7. At tournaments, galas, festivals or friendly internationals, the weigh-in, if desired, may be arranged earlier than one hour 15 minutes before the competition by mutual agreement between the countries concerned, but if a lifter wishes to attempt a world record he shall be reweighed one hour before the competition.

8. When two lifters register the same weight at the weigh-in preceding a competition and they reach the same total, they shall be reweighed to determine the winner. If again, they weigh the same after the competition, they shall be classified equal and shall each receive an award. The next place in line will not be awarded, and the next best competitor shall be ranked after that. The same procedure shall be used should a record be set under the same conditions.

D. Competitive Lifts
Deep Knee Bend (Squat)

1. The lifter must assume an upright position with the top of the bar not more than one inch below the top of the deltoids, the bar across the shoulders in a horizontal position, hands gripping the bar, feet flat on the platform. Upon removing the bar from the racks, the lifter must move backward to establish his position. He shall wait in this position for the referee's signal, which shall be given as soon as the lifter is motionless and the bar is properly positioned. The use of a wedge at the heels or toes is forbidden.

2. After the referee's signal, the lifter shall bend the knees and lower the body until the tops of the thighs are below parallel with the platform. The lifter shall recover at will, without double bouncing to an upright position, knees locked, and wait for the referee's signal to replace the bar, which shall be given when the lifter is absolutely motionless. The lifter must make a bona fide attempt to return the bar to the rack. The top of the thighs shall be defined as being the point at the hip joint that bends when the body is lowered. This point shall develop a parallel relationship with the top of the knee. This refers to the surface of the leg at the hip joint that bends when the body is lowered.

3. The apparatus used shall be of IPF standards. Padding may be applied to the bar only, but it must not exceed 30 cm. in width and 5 cm. in thickness. The lifter shall remove the bar from the racks preparatory to the lift.

4. The lifter must face the front of the platform.

5. The lifter may not hold the collars, sleeves, or the plates at any time during the performance of the lift. However, the side of the hand may contact the inside of the inner collars.

Causes for Disqualification of the Squat

1. During the lift, failure to wait for the referee's signals.
2. Any change of the position of the hands on the bar.
3. More than one recovery attempt.
4. Failure to assume an upright position at the start and completion of the lift.
5. Failure to lower the body until the tops of the thighs are below parallel.
6. Any shifting of the feet during the performance of the lift.·
7. Any shifting of the bar on the body during the performance of the lift.
8. Any touching of the bar by the spotters before the referee's signal.
9. Any raising of the heels or toes.
10. Any touching of the legs with the elbows or upper arms.

Bench Press

1. The lifter may elect to assume one of the following two positions on the bench, which must be maintained during the lift. (A) with head, trunk, and legs extended on the bench, knees locked, heels on a second bench, or (B) with head, trunk (including buttocks) extended on the bench, feet flat on the floor.
2. The referee's signal shall be given when the bar is absolutely motionless at the chest.
3. After the referee's signal, the bar is pressed vertically to straight arms length and held motionless for the referee's signal to replace the bar.
4. The width of the bench shall be not less than 25 cm. or more than 30 cm. The height shall not be less than 35 cm. and not more than 45 cm. The length shall be not less than 1 meter 22 cm. and shall be flat and level.
5. The spacing of the hands shall not exceed 81 cm. measured between the forefingers.
6. If the lifter's costume and the bench top are not of a sufficient color contrast to enable the officials to detect a possible raising of the buttocks, the bench top shall be covered accordingly.
7. In this lift the referees shall station themselves at the best points of vantage.
8. For those lifters who elect to use position (B) and whose feet do not touch the floor, the platform may be built up to provide firm footing.
9. A maximum of four and a minimum of two spotter-loaders shall be mandatory, however the lifter may enlist one or more of the official spotter-loaders to assist him in removing the bar from the racks.

Causes for Disqualification for the Bench Press

1. During the uplifting, any change of the elected lifting position.
2. Any raising or shifting of the lifter's head, shoulders, buttocks, or legs from the bench, or movement of the feet.
3. Any heaving or bouncing of the bar from the chest.
4. Allowing the bar to sink excessively into the lifter's chest prior to the uplift.
5. Any uneven extension of the arms.
6. Stopping of the bar during the press proper.
7. Any touching of the bar by the spotters, before the referee's signal to replace the bar.
8. Failure to wait for the referee's signal.
9. Touching against the uprights of the bench with the feet.
10. Touching the shoulders against the uprights of the bench.
11. Allowing the bar to touch the uprights of the bench during the lift.

Deadlift

1. The bar must be laid horizontally in front of the lifter's feet, gripped with an optional grip with both hands, and uplifted with one continuous motion until the lifter is standing erect. At the completion of the lift, the knees must be locked and the shoulders thrust back. The referee's signal shall indicate the time when the bar is held motionless in the final position.

Causes for Disqualification for the Deadlift

1. Any stopping of the bar before it reaches the final position.
2. Failure to stand erect.
3. Failure to lock the knees.
4. Supporting the bar on the thighs.
5. Any raising of the bar or any deliberate attempt to do so shall count as an attempt.
6. Any shifting of the feet during the performance of the lift.
7. Any raising of the heels or toes.
8. Lowering the bar before the referee's signal to do so.
9. Allowing the bar to return to the platform without maintaining control with both hands.

E. Order of Competition

1. The platform for powerlifting shall measure a maximum of 4 m. × 4 m. and a minimum of 3 m. × 3 m.
2. The chief referee shall be seated in front of the platform. The three referees may seat themselves according to the best points of vantage.
3. The bar is loaded progressively, the lifter taking the lowest weight lifting first. In no case can the bar be reduced to a lighter weight when the lifter has performed a lift with the weight announced. The lifters, or their coaches, must therefore observe the progressive loading and be ready to make their attempt at the weight they have chosen.
4. In an international match between two individuals or two nations, contested in separate categories, the lifters may lift in alternate succession. The lifter taking the lighter weight shall lift first and that order shall be maintained throughout that particular lift.
5. One or more officials shall be appointed by the organizers. Their duties are: (A) Arranging, as necessary, the attempts chosen by the competitors and ensuring their order and progression. (B) When necessary, drawing lots for the competitors.
6. When several lifters declare their wish to take their first attempt or any one lift with a bar of the same weight, they shall lift in the order determined by the drawing of lots at the weigh-in. The lifter whose name is drawn first must consequently lift first until the last attempt on this lift, if the progression of these lifters remains the same. If, during the following lift, the same lifters want to take the bar of the same weight, the lifter who went first in the preceding lift must this time go last. If the same case is repeated for the following lift, the same procedure will follow as before.
7. A lifter taking his first attempt must precede lifters taking their second or third attempts with the same weight. Similarly, a lifter taking his second attempt must precede any lifter wanting to take his third attempt with the same weight.
8. In international competitions (except for a record attempt made outside the competition), the weight of the bars used must always be a multiple of 2.5 kg. The progression is by at least 5 kg. at a time, and a request for 2.5 kg., only, indicates the last attempt. The weight shall be announced in kilograms.

9. The weights announced by the speaker must be immediately displayed on an easily visible scoreboard.

10. A delay of one minute shall be allowed to competitors from the calling of their name to the starting of the attempt. If the delay exceeds one minute, it shall eliminate the attempt. The clock shall stop when the lifter starts the lift proper. A timekeeper shall be appointed. A lifter taking the second and third attempts following himself, will be given three minutes to start the lift, with a warning at the end of two minutes.

11. During any competition organized on a platform or stage, nobody other than the members of the jury, the officiating referees, the managers, and the lifters engaged in the category being contested shall be allowed around the platform or on the stage.

12. The chief referee is the sole judge of the decision to take in the case of an error in the loading of the bar, or of incorrect announcing by the speaker.

Examples

a. If the bar is loaded to a lighter weight than that requested by the lifter, the successful attempt must be cancelled and a further attempt granted to the lifter at the weight actually chosen by him.

b. If the bar is loaded to a heavier weight than that stated and requested by the lifter and the lift is good, he shall grant this attempt at the weight just succeeded and shall reduce the weight if other lifters have asked to lift with a lower weight. If the attempt is unsuccessful, he shall cause the weight to be reduced to that originally chosen by the lifter and shall grant him a further attempt at this weight.

c. If the loading is not the same on each side of the bar, or any change in the bar or discs happens during the execution of a lift, or the platform is disarranged, he shall cancel the attempt missed because of this and shall grant a further attempt.

d. When the loading error happens during the second attempt of a lift and the progression, because of this error, is only 2.5 kg., the attempt, if recognized as a good lift shall be granted to the lifter if he wants it, but shall cancel the third attempt. If on the contrary, the lifter wants to take advantage of his third attempt, the second attempt, because of the error, will be cancelled, and a further attempt shall be granted to the lifter at the weight originally chosen by him. First attempt 80 kg., second attempt requested 85 kg., the bar is loaded in error to 82.5 kg. The decision is either to cancel the third attempt if the lifter agrees or to grant another attempt at 85 kg.

e. If the speaker makes a mistake in announcing a weight lighter or heavier than that requested by a competitor, the chief referee must make the same decisions as for errors in loading.

f. In certain contests where the lifters are not obliged to remain near the platform, therefore finding it impossible to follow the progress of the attempts of the other competitors, the weight must be similarly reduced in a case where the speaker has omitted to call the lifter at the time when the latter would normally have taken his attempt.

13. These decisions must be given to the speaker who will then make an appropriate announcement.
14. Zero in one of the lifts eliminates the lifter from the contest.
15. There shall be no wrapping and adjustment of costume, except the belt, in the designated lifting perimeter.

Referees

 1. The referees are three in number.
 2. One of them, called the chief referee, gives the signals required in all three lifts. He must give an audible and visible signal at the completion of each lift.
 3. When the lifter has replaced the bar on the platform, it is the chief referee who will make known the referee's decision. This will be done with a system of lights. These lights must only light up when all switches are pressed by the three referees and not separately.
 4. The chief referee shall be seated in front of the platform. The three referees may seat themselves according to the best points of vantage.
 5. Before the contest the referees must ascertain:
    a. That the platform and equipment are according to the rules.
    b. That the scales work accurately and correctly.
    c. That all competitors weigh in within the limit of their category during the one hour permitted.
    d. That the costume of the lifters is correct as well as the belts, bandages, etc.
 6. During the contest the referees must ascertain:
    a. That the weight of the bar agrees with that announced by the speaker.
    b. That nobody but the lifter handles the bar during the execution of the lift.
 7. If one of the side referees sees a serious fault during the performance of a lift, he must raise his hand to call attention to the fault. If there is agreement from the other side or from the chief referee himself, this constitutes a majority decision opinion and the chief referee shall stop the lift and signal the lifter to replace the bar.
 8. During the contests they are called upon to adjudicate, the referees must not receive any document concerning the progress of the championship. They must abstain from any commentary.
 9. The referees shall be selected by the technical committee. They must have proved their competence at international meetings and national championships.
10. Drawing of lots must decide which category they shall referee. Two referees of the same nation cannot be selected to adjudicate in the same category in a contest of more than two nations.
11. The selection of a referee to a position of chief referee does not prevent his selection as a side referee in another category, in the case of insufficient Category 1 referees.
12. Each country may nominate a maximum of three referees to serve at World Championships. All referees must be of international standards, approved by the IPF.
13. Referees and members of the jury shall wear uniform dress which shall consist of: Dark blue or black blazer, grey trousers and an IPF badge worn on the pocket of

the blazer. Only the IPF badge shall be worn on the blazer. In very hot weather and subject to the permission of the jury, referees may wear white shirt and grey trousers.

14. A candidate for Category II must be a national referee in good standing in his own country and be recommended by his National Secretary. He must take the Category II written exam at a world championship, continental championship, regional game, international tournament, national championship, or national clinic. The test must be given only after a complete comprehensive rules clinic and the applicant must make a passing score of 90 percent or more.

15. A candidate for Category I referee must be a Category II referee in good standing for a period of at least one year. He must take the Category I practical at a world championship, continental championship, regional game, or international tournament. The applicant is to be scrutinized by the jury which must consist of three Category I referees. The applicant must be scrutinized while serving as chief referee and must adjudicate over at least 100 attempts during his exam. He must make a score of 90 percent in all of his decisions. His decisions will be compared to those of the jury members and not those of his fellow referees. Test score sheets shall be scored by the General Secretary and credentials issued accordingly through the submitting federation.

F. World Records

1. At world, continental championships, regional games, international tournaments, and national championships, world records will be accepted without weighing the barbell or the lifter provided that the lifter has weighed in correctly before the competition according to the IPF rules for the competition and provided that the referees or the chairman of the technical committee have checked the weight of the barbell before the competition.

2. At all other competitions the barbell shall be weighed immediately after the record lift, and the lifter shall present himself backstage for inspection by the three referees judging his category.

3. The conditions to be fulfilled for the registration of a record are as follows:
    a. The only records that shall be recognized are those which have been set at a competition in a member nation recognized by the IPF and accepted by three referees, all of whom must hold an IPF international referee's card.
    b. The decisions of the judges will be in the affirmative as long as at least two of the referees have displayed white lights or a positive signal.
    c. The good faith and competence of referees of all member nations cannot be doubted so the recognition of a world record can be assured by referees of the same nation.

4. The conditions to be fulfilled for registration of a record are as follows:
    a. If the record is not set in in one of the official competitions listed above, the three referees must weigh the barbell immediately after the record lift.
    b. The three referees must sign a written report affirming on their honor:
        1. The validity of the lift.
        2. The name and nation of the lifter.
        3. The lifter's bodyweight.
        4. The absolutely precise weight of the barbell.
        5. The place of the performance.
        6. The date and title of the competition during which the record was broken.

7. In the case of junior lifters, their date of birth must also be given.
8. Proof that the scales were certified to accuracy by the proper authority.
9. This report must be signed by the three referees and the chairman of the jury or the secretary of the national federation.

5. The report must be sent to the General Secretary of the IPF within one calendar month of the date of record. The record will only be ratified after the General Secretary has received the written report within the specified time limit.

6. When during an international competition, a lifter succeeds with a lift that is within 10 kg. of a world record, he may be granted a fourth attempt outside the competition if the jury permits it. In no case will a lifter be granted a further attempt.

7. A lifter who wishes to attempt a world record which is not a multiple of 2.5 kg. can only do so as a fourth attempt outside the competition. There is no need to weigh the barbell or the lifter again if the lift accords with other rules for world records.

8. Only those lifters actually competing in the competition may attempt records outside the competition. Additional lifters shall not be brought in specially for the purpose of attempting records on individual lifts. When two lifters break the same record, either on an individual lift or on the total, during the course of the competition, it is the lighter lifter who will be the new record holder. A national or international record will only be valid if it exceeds by at least 500 gram the previous record. Fractions of less than 500 gram must be ignored. Example: 87.700 is registered as 87.500.

9. There is an official world record for the total of three lifts. It is only recognized if it is set during national, international, or other matches under the IPF rules and in a member nation. The bar and the lifter will not be weighed after the competition but a written report similar to the one required for individual records must be drawn up and signed by the three referees. The record will only be valid for the category corresponding to the official weigh-in and without taking into account any extra attempts. Not only world records, but also continental and regional games records broken under the same conditions as world records shall be recognized and confirmed in the same manner.

G. Team Scoring

1. Point scoring for all world, continental, and national championships shall be: 12, 9, 8, 7, 6, 5, 4, 3, 2, 1. Point scoring for all other competitions shall be: 5, 3, 1.
2. Only member national affiliates of the IPF may score points in sanctioned competition.
3. The maximum number of team members in a contest is ten.
4. Teams shall be nominated to the Secretary of the IPF at least 21 days before the date of the championship.
5. Team awards shall be given for the first three places.
6. In the case of a tie, the same procedure used to determine placing of lifters shall be used in determining team points.
7. In the case of a tie in the classification of teams of countries, the team having the largest number of first places shall be ranked first. In the case of two countries having the same number of first places, the one having the most second places shall be classified first, and so on through ten places.

index